# Contents

# Country Breakfast Cereal

**Preparation Time**: 5 minutes

**Cooking Time**: 40 minutes

**Servings**: 6

**Ingredients**:

- 1 cup brown rice, uncooked
- ½ cup raisins, seedless
- 1 tsp cinnamon, ground
- ¼ Tbsp peanut butter
- 2 ¼ cups water
- Honey, to taste
- Nuts, toasted

**Directions**:

1. Combine rice, butter, raisins, and cinnamon in a saucepan. Add 2 ¼ cups water. Bring to boil.
2. Simmer covered for 40 minutes until rice is tender.  Fluff with fork. Add honey and nuts to taste.

**Nutrition**: 160 Calories34g Carbohydrates1.5g Fats3g Protein

# Oatmeal Fruit Shake

**Preparation Time**: 10 minutes

**Cooking Time**: 0 minutes

**Servings**: 2

**Ingredients**:

- 1 cup oatmeal, already prepared, cooled
- 1 apple, cored, roughly chopped
- 1 banana, halved
- 1 cup baby spinach
- 2 cups coconut water
- 2 cups ice, cubed
- ½ tsp ground cinnamon
- 1 tsp pure vanilla extract

**Directions**:

1. Transfer all **ingredients** to a blender. Blend it from low to high pulse until smooth.

**Nutrition**:

270 Calories58g Carbohydrates1.5g Fats5g Protein

# Amaranth Banana Breakfast Porridge

**Preparation Time**: 10 minutes

**Cooking Time**: 25 minutes

**Servings**: 8

**Ingredients**:

- 2 cup amaranth
- 2 cinnamon sticks
- 4 bananas, diced
- 2 Tbsp chopped pecans
- 4 cups water

**Directions**:

1. Combine the amaranth, water, and cinnamon sticks, and banana in a pot. Cover and let simmer around 25 minutes. Remove from heat and discard the cinnamon. Places into bowls, and top with pecans.

**Nutrition**:

330 Calories62g Carbohydrates6g Fats10g Protein

# Alkaline Chocolate Green Thickie

**Preparation Time**: 15 minutes

**Cooking Time**: 20 minutes

**Serving**: 4

**Ingredients**:

- 1-3 finely diced cucumber
- 2 cups of spinach
- 1 teaspoon of powdered wheatgrass juice
- 2 cups of a deep - freeze. Broccoli
- 30g of powdered protein rice, vanilla
- 1 tablespoon of powdered cocoa
- 1 cup of coconut milk
- 1 spoon of rice malt syrup
- 1-2 spoons of extracted vanilla

**Directions**:

1. Combine all the **ingredients** and mix until it is smooth and creamy. Serve in a glass or bowl and have a yummy breakfast.

**Nutrition**:

205 calories49g protein21g fiber4g sugar

# Cleansing Smoothie Bowl

**Preparation Time**: 15 minutes

**Cooking Time**: 5 minutes

**Servings**: 3

**Ingredients**:

- 1-3 finely diced cucumber
- 75g of baby spinach
- 2 big-leaves kale
- 1 cup of sprouted alfalfa
- 2 teaspoon of Chia seeds
- 2 teaspoons of almond butter
- 1 serve of uncooked broccoli
- 1 small size avocado
- 1 spoon of vanilla
- 1 cup of coconut milk

**Directions**:

1. Combine all the **ingredients** and mix until it is smooth and creamy. Serve in a bowl and have a sumptuous breakfast.

**Nutrition**: 96 calories24g protein14g fiber5g sugar

# Breakfast Quinoa

**Preparation Time**: 20 minutes

**Cooking Time**: 15 minutes

**Servings**: 3

**Ingredients**:

- 1 cup of boiled quinoa
- 1½ cups of boiled broccoli
- 1 tablespoon of flaxseed oil
- 2 tablespoons of saturated almonds
- Pure sea salt and a handful of parsley

**Directions**:

1. Boil quinoa using the ratio of water to quinoa as 3:1. Boil the broccoli on low heat. Leave almonds in water for about 12 hours before cooking. Mix all **ingredients** in a salad bowl and eat your meal!

**Nutrition**: 114 calories24g protein12g fiber8g sugar

# Spelt Flour Pancake

**Preparation Time**: 10 minutes

**Cooking Time**: 5 minutes

**Servings**: 2

**Ingredients**:

- 2 cups of flour, spelt
- 1 egg
- 1 cup of Coconut milk
- 2 tablespoon of olive oil
- 3 cups of alkaline water
- 2 tablespoons Ground cinnamon

**Directions**:

1. Get a bowl, add the flour, coconut milk, egg and whisk. Pour in the water and whisk continuously for a beautiful and smooth mix. Get a baking pan in an oven with low heat, put some olive oil in the pan.
2. After a minute, pour the prepared flour and spread in circles.  Cook for 1:30 - 2 minutes.
3. Serve warm and enjoy.

**Nutrition**: 97 calories18g fiber34g protein5g sugar

# Crunchy Quinoa Meal

**Preparation Time**: 5 minutes

**Cooking Time**: 25 minutes

**Serving**: 2

**Ingredients**:

- 3 cups coconut milk
- 1 cup quinoa, rinsed
- 1/8 teaspoon ground cinnamon
- 1 cup raspberry
- ½ cup chopped coconuts

**Directions**:

1. Add milk into a saucepan and bring to a boil over high heat. Add quinoa to the milk and again bring it to a boil. Let it simmer for 15 minutes, on low heat until milk is reduced. Stir in cinnamon and mix well. Cover and cook for 8 minutes until milk is completely absorbed. Add raspberry and cook for 30 seconds. Serve and enjoy.

**Nutrition**:

271 Calories3.7g Fat54g Carbs3.5g Fiber6.5g Protein

# Coconut Pancakes

**Preparation Time**: 5 minutes

**Cooking Time**: 15 minutes

**Serving**: 4

**Ingredients**:

- 1 cup coconut flour
- 2 tablespoons arrowroot powder
- Teaspoon baking powder
- 1 cup coconut milk
- 3 tablespoons coconut oil

**Directions**:

1. Mix all dry **ingredients** in a medium container.  Add coconut milk and 2 tablespoons coconut oil. Mix well. Melt a teaspoon coconut oil in a skillet. Pour a ladle of the batter into the skillet and swirl the pan to spread it into a smooth pancake. Cook for 3 minutes on low heat until firm.
2. Flip the pancake and cook for another 2 to 3 minutes until golden brown. Cook more pancakes using the remaining batter. Serve.

**Nutrition**:

377 Calories14.9g Fat60.7g Carbs6.4g Protein1.4g Fiber

# Blueberry Porridge

**Preparation Time**: 5 minutes

**Cooking Time**: 25 minutes

**Serving**: 2

**Ingredients**:

- 2 cups coconut milk
- 1 cup quinoa, rinsed
- 1/8 teaspoon ground cinnamon
- 1 cup (1/2 pint) fresh blueberries

**Directions**:

1. Boil coconut milk in a saucepan over high heat. Add quinoa to the milk and again bring it to a boil. Let it simmer for 15 minutes on low heat until milk is reduced.
2. Stir in cinnamon and mix well. Cover and cook for 8 mines until milk is completely absorbed. Add blueberries and cook for 30 seconds. Serve and enjoy.

**Nutrition**:

271 Calories3.7g Fat54g Carbs6.5g Protein3.5g Fiber

# Alkaline Blueberry Breakfast Cake

**Preparation Time**: 15 minutes

**Cooking Time**:  7 hours

**Servings**:  6

**Ingredients**:

- 1 tablespoon grapeseed oil
- 3/4 cup spelt flour
- 3/4 cup teff flour
- 1/4 teaspoon sea salt
- 1 cup coconut milk
- 1/3 cup agave
- 1/2 cup fresh blueberries

**Directions**:

1. Grease a cake pan with grapeseed oil and line with parchment paper. Set aside. Make sure that the cake pan will fit inside the Instant Pot. In a bowl, mix together the spelt and teff flour. Add the salt and stir to combine everything.
2. In another bowl, combine the milk and agave. Stir the wet **ingredients** to the dry **ingredients** and fold until well-combined or until the lumps are formed.
3. Add in the blueberries last. Pour the batter into the prepared cake pan. Place in the Instant Pot and close the lid. Make sure that the vent is not set to the sealing position.
4. Adjust the **cooking time** to 7 hours.

**Nutrition**: 293 Calories7.4g Protein39.8g Carbs7.6g Sugar13g Fat:

# Teff Sausages

**Preparation Time**: 10 minutes

**Cooking Time**:  25 minutes

**Servings**: 6

**Ingredients**:

- 1-1/2 cup teff grains, raw
- 1/2 cup chickpea flour
- 1/4 cup diced onions
- 1 tablespoon green peppers, diced
- 2 tablespoon ground sage
- 1 teaspoon oregano
- 1 teaspoon salt
- 1/2 teaspoon dill, chopped
- Grapeseed oil for frying

**Directions**:

1. Place the teff grains in the Instant Pot and pour 2 cups of water. Set it into sealing position.
2. Press the Multigrain button and adjust the **cooking time** to 15  minutes until the grains are cooked.
3. Once the timer sets off, do natural pressure release, and remove the grains. Place grains in a bowl to cool. Set aside. Meanwhile, clean the inner pot and place back into the Instant Pot.
4. To the cooked teff grains, add the chickpea flour, onions, green peppers, sage, oregano, salt, and dill. Using your hands, mix all **ingredients** and form small logs. Place in the fridge to set for at least 30 minutes.
5. Heat grapeseed oil in the Instant Pot. Press the Sauté button. Place the sausages in the Instant Pot and carefully roll the sausages until the surfaces turn golden. Serve immediately.

**Nutrition**:

215 Calories8.5g Protein41.5g Carbs2.3g Sugar1.8g Fat

# Alkaline Breakfast Biscuits

**Preparation Time**: 10 minutes

**Cooking Time**:  4 hours

**Servings**: 6

**Ingredients**:

- 2 cups spelt flour
- 3/4 cup coconut milk
- 3/4 cup grapeseed oil
- 1 teaspoon sea salt

**Directions**:

1. Transfer all the **ingredients** in bowl and mix it well until it creates a crumbly dough.
2. On a flat working surface roll the dough to 1" thick then fold over dough on top of itself before rolling again. Do this for a few times to create many layers within the biscuit.
3. Slice the biscuit. Place a parchment paper at the bottom of the Instant Pot.
4. Gently place the biscuits in the prepared pot. To increase the cooking capacity, place a trivet on top and line with parchment. Place a few biscuits on top of the prepared trivet.
5. Close the lid but do not set the vent to the Sealing position.
6. Press the Slow Cook button and adjust the **cooking time** to 4 hours.

**Nutrition**:

518 Calories13.7g Protein63.6g Carbs7.5g Sugar26.5g Fat

# Amaranth Porridge

**Preparation Time**: 5 minutes

**Cooking Time**: 30 minutes

**Serving**: 2

**Ingredients**:

- 2 cups coconut milk
- 2 cups water
- 1 cup amaranth
- 2 tablespoons coconut oil
- 1 tablespoon ground cinnamon

**Directions**:

1. Mix milk with water in a medium saucepan. Bring the mixture to a boil.  Stir in amaranth then reduce the heat to low. Cook on low simmer for 30 minutes with occasional stirring.
2. Turn off the heat. Stir in cinnamon and coconut oil. Serve warm.

**Nutrition**:

434 Calories35g Fat27g Carbs6.7g Protein3.6g Fiber

# Banana Barley Porridge

**Preparation Time**: 5 minutes

**Cooking Time**: 30 minutes

**Serving**: 2

**Ingredients**:

- 1 cup unsweetened coconut milk, divided
- 1 small banana, peeled and sliced
- ½ cup barley
- 3 drops liquid stevia
- ¼ cup coconuts, chopped

**Directions**:

1. Mix barley with half coconut milk and stevia in a bowl and mix well. Cover and refrigerate for about 6 hours. Mix the barley mixture with coconut milk in a saucepan. Cook for 5 minutes on medium heat.
2. Top with chopped coconuts and banana slices. Serve.

**Nutrition**: 434 Calories35g Fat26g Carbs6.7g Protein

# Zucchini Muffins

**Preparation Time**: 10 minutes

**Cooking Time**: 25 minutes

**Serving**: 16

**Ingredients**:

- 1 tablespoon ground flaxseed
- 3 tablespoons water
- ¼ cup walnut butter
- 3 small-medium over-ripe bananas
- 2 small zucchinis, grated
- ½ cup coconut milk
- 1 teaspoon vanilla extract
- 2 cups coconut flour
- 1 tablespoon baking powder
- 1 teaspoon cinnamon
- ¼ teaspoon sea salt

**Optional add-ins:**

- ¼ cup chocolate chips and/or walnuts

**Directions**:

1. Set your oven to 375 degrees F. Grease a muffin tray with cooking spray. Mix flaxseed with water in a bowl.
2. Mash bananas in a glass bowl and stir in all the remaining **ingredients**. Mix well and divide the mixture into the muffin tray. Bake for 25 minutes. Serve.

**Nutrition**:

127 Calories6.6g Fat13g Carbs0.7g Protein

# Millet Porridge

**Preparation Time**: 10 minutes

**Cooking Time**: 20 minutes

**Serving**: 2

**Ingredients**:

- Pinch of sea salt
- 1 tablespoon coconuts, chopped finely
- ½ cup unsweetened coconut milk
- ½ cup millet, rinsed and drained
- 1½ cups water
- 3 drops liquid stevia

**Directions**:

1. Sauté millet in a non-stick skillet for 3 minutes. Stir in salt and water. Let it boil then reduce the heat. Cook for 15 minutes then stirs in remaining **ingredients**. Cook for another 4 minutes.
2. Serve with chopped nuts on top.

**Nutrition**: 219 Calories4.5g Fat38.2g Carbs6.4g Protein5g Fiber

# Grain-Free Muesli

**Preparation Time**: 10 minutes

**Cooking Time**: 25 minutes

**Servings**: 2

**Ingredients**:

- 1 cup of uncooked almonds
- 1 cup of uncooked pumpkin seeds
- 1 tablespoon of mashed walnuts
- 1 tablespoon of Chia seeds
- 1 cup of natural coconut milk
- 1 teaspoon of unprocessed vanilla extracts
- 1 teaspoon of rice malt syrup
- 2 teaspoons of cinnamon, ground

**Directions**:

1. Put pumpkin seeds, walnuts, and almonds in a clean bowl. Put enough water and place it in a refrigerator for a night.
2. Clean the almonds, pumpkin seeds, and walnuts. Add it to a container holding coconut milk, vanilla, Chia seeds, and cinnamon. Combine adequately and have an excellent breakfast.

**Nutrition**: 105 calories36g protein20g fiber4g sugar

# Chia Seed Pudding

**Preparation Time**: 10 minutes

**Cooking Time**: 5 minutes

**Servings**: 2

**Ingredients**:

- 1 small cup of chia seeds
- 1 cup of natural coconut milk
- 2 tablespoons of saturated almonds
- 2 teaspoons of vanilla
- 1 small cup of berries, blue

**Directions**:

1. Put all **ingredients** in a container and combine adequately. Keep in the refrigerator overnight.
2. Serve and enjoy your breakfast.

**Nutrition**: 88 calories25g protein12g fiber8g sugar

# Sprouted Toast with Creamy Avocado and Sprouts

**Preparation Time**: 10 minutes

**Cooking Time**: 15 minutes

**Servings**: 3

**Ingredients**:

- 2 small sized bread sprouts
- 1 cup of finely cut tomatoes
- 2 moderate size avocados
- 1 small cup of alfalfa
- Pure sea salt and bell pepper

**Directions**:

1. Add the avocado, alfalfa, and tomatoes to the bread and season to taste with pure sea salt and pepper.  Have a sumptuous breakfast with any freshly extracted juice of your choice .

**Nutrition**: 82 calories15g fiber30g protein7g sugar

# Scrambled Turmeric Tofu

**Preparation Time**: 5 minutes

**Cooking Time**: 15 minutes

**Servings**: 4

**Ingredients**:

- 1 crumbled serve of tofu
- 1 small cup of finely chopped onions
- 1 teaspoon of the fresh parsley
- 1 teaspoon of coconut oil
- 1 cup of soft spinach
- 1 small teaspoon of Turmeric
- 2 avocado serves
- 75g of tomatoes
- 1 small spoon of roasted paprika

**Directions**:

1. Make tofu crumbs with your hands and keep it separately. Sauté diced onions in oil till it softens.
2. Put your tofu, tomatoes, and other seasonings and combine till tofu is well prepared.  Add veggies and stir. Serve in a bowl alongside  some avocado.

**Nutrition**: 91 calories12g fiber30g protein8g sugar

# Breakfast Salad

**Preparation Time**: 5 minutes

**Cooking Time**: 15 minutes

**Servings**: 3

**Ingredients**:

- 1 cup of finely diced kale
- 1 cup of cabbage, red and Chinese
- 2 tablespoons of coconut oil
- 1 cup of spinach
- 2 moderate avocados
- 1.2kg of chickpeas sprout
- 2 tablespoons of sunflower seed sprouts
- Pure sea salt (seasoning)
- Bell pepper (seasoning)
- Lemon juice (seasoning)

**Directions**:

1. Add spinach, Chinese and red cabbage, kale, coconut oil, in a container.  Add seasoning to taste and mix adequately.  Add other **ingredients** and mix.

**Nutrition**: 112 calories28g protein10g fiber1g sugar

# Green Goddess Bowl with Avocado Cumin Dressing

**Preparation Time**: 10 minutes

**Cooking Time**: 20 minutes

**Servings**: 4

**Ingredients**:

- 3 heaping cups of finely sliced kale
- 1 small cup of diced broccoli florets
- ½ cup of zucchini spiralized noodles
- ½ cup of soaked Kelp noodles
- 3 cups of tomatoes
- 2 tablespoon of hemp seeds
- Tahini dressing **ingredients**:
- 1 small cup of sesame butter
- 1 cup of alkaline water

- 1 cup of freshly extracted lemon
- 1 garlic, finely chopped clove
- ¾ tablespoon of pure sea salt
- 1 spoon of olive oil
- Bell pepper
- Avocado dressing **ingredients**:
- 1 big avocado
- 2 freshly extracted lime
- 1 cup of alkaline water
- 1 tablespoon of olive oil
- Bell pepper
- 1 tablespoon of powdered cumin

**Directions**:

1. Simmer veggies — kale and broccoli for about four minutes. Combine noodles and add avocado cumin dressing. Toss for a while. Add tomatoes and combine well. Put the cooked kale and broccoli in a plate, add Tahini dressing, add noodles and tomatoes. Add a couple of hemp seeds to the whole dish and enjoy it.

**Nutrition**: 109 calories25g protein17g fiber8g sugar

# Quinoa Burrito

**Preparation Time**: 15 minutes

**Cooking Time**: 10 minutes

**Servings**: 1

**Ingredients**:

- 1 cup of quinoa
- 2 cups of black beans
- 4 finely chopped onions, green
- 4 finely chopped garlic
- Two freshly cut limes
- 1 big tablespoon of cumin
- 2 beautifully diced avocado
- 1 small cup of beautifully diced cilantro

**Directions**:

1. Boil quinoa. During this process, put the beans in low heat. Add other **ingredients** to the beans pot and let it mix well for about 15 minutes. Serve quinoa and add the prepared beans.

**Nutrition**: 117 calories27g protein10g fiber2g sugar

# Chickpeas & Mushroom Burgers

**Preparation Time**: 20 minutes

**Cooking Time**: 20 minutes

**Serving**: 4

**Ingredients**:

- 2 Portobello mushrooms, chopped roughly
- ½ cup green bell peppers
- ½ cup white onion, chopped roughly
- 2 cups cooked chickpeas
- ½ cup fresh cilantro
- 2 teaspoons fresh oregano, chopped
- 2 teaspoons onion powder
- ½ teaspoon cayenne powder
- Sea salt, as required
- ¼ cup chickpea flour
- 3 tablespoons grapeseed oil
- 6 cups fresh baby arugula

**Directions**:

1. Transfer all of **ingredients** in a food processor and pulse for about 3 seconds. Make 8 equal-sized patties from mixture.
2. In a large skillet, heat half of the oil over medium-high heat and cook 4 patties for about 4-5 minutes per side. Repeat with the remaining oil and patties. Divide the arugula onto **serving** plates and top each  with 2 burgers.
3. Serve immediately.

**Nutrition**: 278 Calories12.2g Total Fat11.2g Protein31g Carbs7.6g Fiber

# Veggie Burgers

**Preparation Time**: 0 minutes

**Cooking Time**: 6 minutes

**Serving**: 2

**Ingredients**:

- ½ cup fresh kale, tough ribs removed and chopped
- ½ cup green bell peppers, seeded and chopped
- ½ cup onions, chopped
- 1 plum tomato, chopped
- 2 teaspoons fresh oregano, chopped
- 2 teaspoons fresh basil, chopped
- 1 teaspoon dried dill
- 1 teaspoon onion powder
- ½ teaspoon ginger powder

- ½ teaspoon cayenne powder
- Sea salt, as required
- 1 cup chickpeas flour
- ¼-½ cup spring water
- 2 tablespoons grapeseed oil
- 3 cups fresh arugula

**Directions**:

1. Mix in the vegetables, herbs, spices and salt in a bowl. Add the flour and mix well. Gradually, add in the water until a thick mixture is formed. Make desired-sized patties from the mixture. Cook the oil over medium-high heat and cook the patties for about 2-3 minutes per side. Divide the arugula onto **serving** plates and top each with 2 burgers.
2. Serve immediately.

**Nutrition**: 354 Calories17.8g Total Fat13g Protein38.4g Carbs8.1g Fiber

# Falafel with Tzatziki Sauce

**Preparation Time**: 20 minutes

**Cooking Time**: 12 minutes

**Serving**: 8

**Ingredients**:

- For Falafel
- pound dry chickpeas
- 1 small onion
- ¼ cup fresh parsley, chopped
- 4 garlic cloves, peeled
- 1½ tablespoons chickpea flour
- Sea salt, as required
- ½ teaspoon cayenne powder
- ½ cup grapeseed oil
- For Tzatziki Sauce
- ½ cup Brazil nuts
- ½ cup spring water
- ¼ cup cucumber, chopped
- 1 tablespoon fresh key lime juice
- 1 garlic clove, minced
- 1 teaspoon fresh dill
- Pinch of sea salt
- For **Serving**
- 12 cups fresh arugula

**Directions**:

1. For falafel: in a food processor, add all the **ingredients** and pulse until well combined and coarse meal like mixture forms. Transfer the falafel mixture into a bowl. With a plastic wrap, cover the bowl and refrigerate for about 1-2 hours. With 2 tablespoons of the mixture, make balls.
2. Cook the oil at 375 degrees in a skillet. Add the falafels in 2 batches and cook for about 5-6 minutes or until golden brown from all aides.  Meanwhile, for tzatziki: in a blender, add all the **ingredients** and pulse until smooth. With a slotted spoon, transfer the falafels onto a paper towel-lined plate to drain. Divide the arugula and falafels onto **serving** plates evenly.
3. Serve alongside the tzatziki.

**Nutrition**: 283 Calories9.6g Total Fat13.3g Protein38.8g Carbs11.3g Fiber

# Veggie Balls in Tomato Sauce

**Preparation Time**: 20 minutes

**Cooking Time**: 15 minutes

**Serving**: 8

**Ingredients**

- 1½ cups cooked chickpeas
- 2 cups fresh button mushrooms
- ½ cup onions, chopped
- ¼ cup green bell peppers, seeded and chopped
- 2 teaspoons oregano
- 2 teaspoons fresh basil
- 1 teaspoon savory
- 1 teaspoon dried sage
- 1 teaspoon dried dill
- 1 tablespoon onion powder
- ½ teaspoon cayenne powder
- ½ teaspoon ginger powder
- Sea salt, as required
- ½-1 cup chickpea flour
- 6 cups homemade tomato sauce
- 2 tablespoons grapeseed oil

**Directions**:

1. In a food processor, add the chickpeas, veggies, herbs and spices and pulse until well combined. Transfer the mixture into a large bowl with flour and mix until well combined. Make desired-sized balls from the mixture.
2. Cook the oil over medium-high heat and let the balls cook in 2 batches for about 4-5 minutes or until golden brown from all sides. In a large pan, add the tomato sauce and veggie balls over medium heat and simmer for about 5 minutes. Serve hot.

**Nutrition**: 159 Calories4.8g Total Fat7.2g Protein23.9g Carbs6g Fiber

# Alkaline Pizza Crust

**Preparation Time**: 15 minutes

**Cooking Time**: 30 minutes

**Servings**: 8

**Ingredients**

- 1 1/2 cup Spelt Flour
- 1 tsp. Powdered onion
- 1 tsp. Oregano
- 2 tsp. Sesame
- 1 tsp. Sea Salt
- 2 tsp. Agave
- 2 tsp. Grapeseed Oil
- 1 cup Spring water

**Directions**

1. Preheat oven at 400 degrees then combine all of the **ingredients** together in a medium sized container, including only 1/2 cup of spring water. Slowly pour water before the dough can be formed into a ball; if too much water is used pour more flour.
2. Coat the baking sheet thinly with grape seed oil, apply flour to your hands and roll the dough out onto the baking sheet. Brush with grape seed oil to the tip of the crust and stab holes with a fork into it. Bake crust for 10-15 minutes.
3. Prepare the pizza sauce with tomato or avocado as the crust bakes. 6. Add the pizza sauce, brazil nut cheese *, mushrooms, chili peppers, and onions after the crust is cooked. 15-20 minutes to bake the pizza. Enjoy your Alkaline Veggie Pizza!
4. Tips: Nut cheese helps to cook the toppings during the baking process. If you don't have some nut cheese, prefer to sauté the  toppings before baking.

**Nutrition**: 186 calories26g protein13g fiber4g sugar

# Vegetable Chili

**Prep time**: 5 minutes

**Cooking time**: 30 minutes

**Servings**: 6

**Ingredients**

- 2 cups black beans, cooked
- 1 medium red bell pepper; deseeded, chopped
- 1 poblano chili; deseeded, chopped
- 2 jalapeño chilies; deseeded, chopped
- 4 tablespoons cilantro, chopped
- 1 large white onion; peeled, chopped

- 1 ½ tablespoon minced garlic
- 1 ½ teaspoon sea salt
- 1 ½ teaspoon cumin powder
- 1 ½ teaspoon red chili powder
- 3 teaspoons lime juice
- 2 tablespoons grapeseed oil
- 2 ½ cups vegetable stock

**Directions**

1. Take a large pot, place it over medium-high heat, add oil and when hot, add onion and cook for 4–5 minutes until translucent. Add bell pepper, jalapeno pepper, poblano chili, and garlic and then cook for 3–4 minutes until veggies turn tender.
2. Season the vegetables with salt, stir in cumin powder and red chili powder, then add chickpeas and pour in vegetable stock. Bring the mixture to a boil, then switch heat to medium-low and simmer the chili for 15–20 minutes until thickened slightly.
3. Then remove the pot from heat, ladle chili stew among six bowls, drizzle with lime juice, garnish with cilantro, and serve.

**Nutrition**: 224.2 Calories42.6g Carbs1.2g Fat12.5g Protein

# Wild Rice and Black Lentils Bowl

**Prep Time**: 10 minutes

**Cooking Time**: 50 minutes

**Servings**: 4

**Ingredients**

- Wild Rice
- 2 cups wild rice, uncooked
- 4 cups spring water
- ½ teaspoon salt
- 2 bay leaves
- Black Lentils
- 2 cups Black Lentils, cooked
- 1 ¾ cups coconut milk, unsweetened
- 2 cups vegetable stock
- 1 teaspoon dried thyme
- 1 teaspoon dried paprika
- ½ of medium purple onion; peeled, sliced
- 1 tablespoon minced garlic
- 2 teaspoons creole seasoning
- 1 tablespoon coconut oil
- Plantains
- 3 large plantains, chopped into ¼-inch-thick pieces

- 3 tablespoons coconut oil
- Brussels Sprouts
- 10 large Brussels sprouts, quartered
- 2 tablespoons spring water
- 1 teaspoon sea salt
- ½ teaspoon ground black pepper

**Directions**

1. Prepare the rice: take a medium pot, place it over medium-high heat, pour in water, and add bay leaves and salt. Bring the water to a boil, then switch heat to medium, add rice, and then cook for 30–45 minutes or more until tender. When done, discard the bay leaves from rice, drain if any water remains in the pot, remove it from heat,  and fluff by using a fork. Set aside until needed.
2. While the rice boils, prepare lentils: take a large pot, place it over medium-high heat and when hot, add onion and cook for 5 minutes or until translucent. Stir garlic into the onion, cook for 2 minutes until fragrant and golden, then add remaining **ingredients** for the lentils and stir until mixed.
3. Bring the lentils to a boil, then switch heat to medium and simmer the lentils for 20 minutes until tender, covering the pot with a lid. When done, remove the pot from heat and set aside until needed. While rice and lentils simmer, prepare the plantains: chop them into ¼-inch-thick pieces.
4. Take a large skillet pan, place it over medium heat, add coconut oil and when it melts, add half of the plantain pieces and cook for 7–10 minutes per side or more until golden-brown. When done, transfer browned plantains to a plate lined with paper towels and repeat with the remaining plantain pieces; set aside until needed.
5. Prepare the sprouts: return the skillet pan over medium heat, add more oil if needed, and then add Brussels sprouts. Toss the sprouts until coated with oil, and then let them cook for 3–4 minutes per side until brown. Drizzle water over sprouts, cover the pan with the lid, and then cook for 3–5 minutes until steamed.
6. Season the sprouts with salt and black pepper, toss until mixed, and transfer sprouts to a plate. Assemble the bowl: divide rice evenly among four bowls and then top with lentils, plantain pieces, and sprouts. Serve immediately.

**Nutrition**: 333 Calories49.2g Carbs10.7g Fat6.2g Protein

# Spaghetti Squash with Peanut Sauce

**Prep Time**: 15 minutes

**Cooking Time**: 15 minutes

**Servings**: 4

**Ingredients**

- 1 cup cooked shelled edamame; frozen, thawed
- 3-pound spaghetti squash
- ½ cup red bell pepper, sliced

- ¼ cup scallions, sliced
- 1 medium carrot, shredded
- 1 teaspoon minced garlic
- ½ teaspoon crushed red pepper
- 1 tablespoon rice vinegar
- ¼ cup coconut aminos
- 1 tablespoon maple syrup
- ½ cup peanut butter
- ¼ cup unsalted roasted peanuts, chopped
- ¼ cup and 2 tablespoons spring water, divided
- ¼ cup fresh cilantro, chopped
- 4 lime wedges

**Directions**

1. Prepare the squash: cut each squash in half lengthwise and then  remove seeds. Take a microwave-proof dish, place squash halves in it cut-side-up, drizzle with 2 tablespoons water, and then microwave at high heat setting for 10–15 minutes until tender.
2. Let squash cool for 15 minutes until able to handle. Use a fork to scrape its flesh lengthwise to make noodles, and then let noodles cool for 10 minutes. While squash microwaves, prepare the sauce: take a medium bowl, add butter in it along with red pepper and garlic, pour in vinegar, coconut aminos, maple syrup, and water, and then whisk until smooth.
3. When the squash noodles have cooled, distribute them evenly among four bowls, top with scallions, carrots, bell pepper, and edamame beans, and then drizzle with prepared sauce. Sprinkle cilantro and peanuts and serve each bowl with a lime wedge.

**Nutrition**: 419 Calories32.8g Carbs24g Fat17.6g Protein

# Butternut Squash Plum Tomato Spaghetti Sauce

**Preparation Time**: 5 minutes

**Cooking Time**: 20 minutes

**Servings**: 4

**Ingredients**:

- ½ butternut squash
- ¼ plum tomato (chopped)
- 1 cup water
- Spices: dash of cayenne pepper, onion, basil, bay leaf, oregano, thyme, savory, coriander, and salt

**Directions**:

1. Add butternut squash cubes to pot, cover with water and boil until squash becomes tender. Remove squash from water. Add squash, tomato, and spices to a blender and blend, slowly add water until you reach desired consistency.  Add to a container, let cool, and refrigerate.

**Nutrition**: 105 calories21g protein12g fiber

# Simply Chayote Squash

**Preparation Time**: 10 minutes

**Cooking Time**: 20 minutes

**Serving**: 1

**Ingredients**:

- 1 chayote squash
- ¼ teaspoon of coconut oil
- Dash of cayenne pepper
- Dash of sea salt

**Directions**:

1. Serves as a light snack or part of a dish. Wash and cut chayote squash in half. The seed can by eaten and it has a nice texture. Add chayote, oil, and enough water to cover the chayote in a saucepan. Boil for 20  minutes until fork can penetrate the squash, but the squash should still maintain some firmness. Remove form water. Season it well with cayenne pepper and salt.

**Nutrition**: 117 calories9.7g fiber14g protein

# Vegetable Medley Sauté

**Preparation Time**: 10 minutes

**Cooking Time**: 15 minutes

**Serving**: 4

**Ingredients**:

- 1 cup mushrooms (sliced)
- 1 zucchini (sliced)
- 1 yellow squash (sliced)
- 1 red pepper (chopped)
- 1 green pepper (chopped)
- 2 plum tomatoes (chopped)
- ½ red onion (finely chopped)
- ½ cup chayote (finely chopped)
- 3 tbsp. grape-seed oil or avocado oil
- ⅛ tsp cayenne pepper
- ⅛ tsp sea salt

**Directions**:

1. Cook the oil in a saucepan over medium heat. Let the oil get hot. Add in mushrooms and onions and sauté for 4 minutes. Add in the rest of the vegetables and spices and sauté for 8-10 minutes.

**Nutrition**: 115 calories4.9g fiber21g protein

# Chickpea Butternut Squash

**Preparation Time**: 10 minutes

**Cooking Time**: 15 minutes

**Serving**: 2

**Ingredients**:

- 15 oz. cooked chickpeas
- 1 ½ section of a butternut squash
- ¼ plum tomato
- ¼ cup coconut milk
- 1 cup water (add more water to make thinner soup)
- Pinch of dill
- Pinch of all spice
- Pinch of cayenne pepper
- ⅛ tsp of sea salt

**Directions**:

1. Add all the **ingredients** to a blender and blend to your desired consistency. Add the blended **ingredients** to a saucepan over a  medium/high flame until it starts to boil or air bubbles rise. Adjust it into low heat and cook for 30 minutes.

**Nutrition**: 110 calories9.7g fiber11g protein

# Lentil Kale Soup

**Preparation Time**: 5 minutes

**Cooking Time**: 15 minutes

**Servings**: 4

**Ingredients**:

- Onion, 1/2
- Zucchinis, 2
- Celery, 1 rib
- Chive, 1 stalk
- tomatoes, 1 cup, diced

- vegetable broth powder, 1 teaspoon, dried
- Sazon seasoning, 1 teaspoon
- red lentils, 1 cup
- Seville orange juice, 1 tablespoon
- alkaline water, 3 cups
- 1 bunch kale

**Directions**:

1. Add all the vegetables to a greased pan. Sauté for 5 minutes then add  broth, tomatoes, and Sazon seasoning. Mix well and stir in red lentils along with water.
2. Cook until lentil is soft and tender. Add kale and cook for 2 minutes. Serve warm with Seville orange slices on top.

**Nutrition**: 301 Calories12.2g Fat15g Carbs28.8g Protein

# Tangy Lentil Soup

**Ingredients**:

- 2 cups red lentils, picked over and rinsed
- 1 serrano Chile pepper, chopped
- 1 large tomato, chopped, roughly
- 1 1 1/2-inch piece ginger, peeled and grated
- 3 cloves chive, finely chopped
- 1/4 teaspoon ground turmeric
- Sea salt, to taste
- Topping
- 1/4 cup coconut yogurt

**Directions**:

1. Add lentils to a pot and with enough water to cover it. Bring the lentils to a boil then reduce the heat. Cook for 10 minutes on low simmer. Stir in all the remaining **ingredients**.
2. Cook until lentils are soft and well mixed. Garnish a dollop of coconut yogurt. Serve.

**Nutrition**: 248 Calories2.4g Fat12.2g Carbs44.3g Protein

# Vegetable Casserole

**Preparation Time**: 5 minutes.

**Cooking Time**: 1 hour and 30 minutes

**Servings**: 6

**Ingredients**:

- 2 large eggplants, peeled and sliced
- Sea salt, to taste
- 2 large cucumbers, diced

- 2 small green peppers, diced
- 1 Small red pepper, diced
- 1 Small yellow pepper, diced
- ¼ lb. green beans, sliced
- ½ cup olive oil
- 2 large sweet onions, Chopped
- 3 cloves chive, crushed
- 2 yellow Squash, cubed
- 20 cherry tomatoes, halved
- ½ teaspoon sea salt
- ¼ teaspoon fresh ground pepper
- ¼ lb. lima beans (Optional)
- A handful of fresh chopped basil (Optional)
- ¼ cup alkaline water
- 1 cup fresh seasoned breadcrumbs

**Directions**:

1. Set your oven to 350 degrees F. Mix eggplant with salt and keep it aside. Heat a greased skillet and sauté eggplant until evenly browned. Transfer the eggplant to a plate.
2. Sauté onions in the same pan until soft. Stir in chive and cook for a minute then turn off the heat. Layer a greased casserole dish with eggplants, green beans, cucumbers, peppers and yellow squash. Add tomatoes, onion mixture, salt, and pepper. Sprinkle seasoned breadcrumbs on top. Bake for 1 hour and 30 minutes. Serve.

**Nutrition**: 372 Calories11.1g Fat0.9g Carbs63.5g Protein0.2g Fiber

# Mushroom Leek Soup

**Preparation Time**: 5 minutes

**Cooking Time**: 8 minutes

**Servings**: 4

**Ingredients**:

- 3 tablespoons vegetable oil, divided
- 2 ¾ cups leeks, finely chopped
- 3 chive stalks, finely minced
- 7 cups assorted mushrooms, cleaned and sliced
- 5 tablespoons coconut flour
- ¾ teaspoon sea salt
- ½ teaspoon ground black pepper
- 1 tablespoon fresh dill, very finely minced (optional)
- 3 cups vegetable broth
- 2/3 cup coconut cream
- ½ cup coconut milk

- 1 ½ tablespoons sherry vinegar

**Directions**:

1. Heat oil in a Dutch oven and sauté chive and leeks until soft. Stir in mushrooms and sauté for 10 minutes. Add flour, pepper, dill, and salt. Mix well and cook for 2 minutes. Pour in broth and cook to boil.
2. Reduce the heat and add the remaining **ingredients**. Serve warm with coconut flour bread.

**Nutrition**: 127 Calories3.5g Fat3.6g Carbs21.5g Protein0.4g Fiber

# Red Lentil Squash Soup

**Preparation Time**: 5 minutes.

**Cooking Time**: 4 minutes.

**Servings**: 4

**Ingredients**:

- 1 yellow onion, chopped
- 2 tablespoons olive oil
- 1 large butternut squash, diced
- 1 1/2 cups red lentils
- 2 teaspoons dried sage
- 7 cups vegetable broth
- mineral sea salt & white or fresh cracked pepper, to taste

**Directions**:

1. Heat oil in a large stockpot. Add onions and cook for 5 minutes. Stir in squash and sage. Cook for 3 to 5 minutes. Add broth, salt, pepper, and lentils. Cook for 30 minutes on low heat.
2. Puree the mixture using a handheld blender. Garnish with cilantro and serve.

**Nutrition**: 323 Calories7.5g Fat21.4g Carbs10.1g Protein

# Butternut Squash Ginger

**Preparation Time**: 10 minutes

**Cooking Time**: 15 minutes

**Serving**: 2

**Ingredients**:

- 1 section of a butternut squash
- ¼ cup coconut milk
- 1 tbsp. coconut oil
- 3 cups water (add more water to make thinner soup)
- 2 tsp minced fresh ginger

- 1 tbsp. date sugar
- ½ cup of diced onions
- 1 tsp finely chopped fresh thyme
- ⅛ tsp of sea salt
- pinch of all spice
- pinch of cayenne pepper

**Directions**:

1. Peel off the skin and seeds from butternut squash, then chop the squash into medium sized cubes. Add cubes to saucepan and cover cubes with water. Boil until squash becomes soft. Remove softened squash from water and discard water.
2. Add butternut squash, coconut milk, and coconut oil to the blender and blend until smooth. Combine the rest of the **ingredients** and 1 cup of water and blend for a few seconds. Transfer mix to saucepan and stir in the remaining 2 cups of water to the desired consistency.  Add more water if wanted.
3. Bring to a boil, reduce heat and let simmer for 15 minutes.

**Nutrition**: 97 calories6.9g fiber14g protein

# Cream of Avocado Mushroom

**Preparation Time**: 5 minutes

**Cooking Time**: 15 minutes

**Serving**: 2-4

**Ingredients**:

- 2 avocados (scoop out flesh and discard skin)
- juice of 1 key lime
- 2 cups hot water
- ⅛ tsp of cayenne pepper
- ⅛ tsp of sea salt
- Dash of clove
- 1 tbsp. coconut oil or grape seed oil
- 1 cup of sliced mushrooms
- 1 red bell pepper (diced)
- ¼ yellow onion (finely chopped)
- 3 plum tomatoes (diced)
- 3 sprigs of fresh thyme leaves

**Directions**:

1. Add hot water, avocados, lime juice, cayenne pepper, sea salt, and all spice in a blender. Pulse until smooth. Heat oil in saucepan over medium and stir in mushrooms, red bell pepper, onion, tomatoes, and thyme until they become soft. Add in avocado mix to the saucepan and simmer for 5 minutes.

**Nutrition**: 99 calories12g protein5.8g fibers

# Vegan Alkaline Ribs

**Preparation Time**: 20 minutes

**Cooking Time**: 35 minutes

**Serving**: 1

**Ingredients**

- 2 portobello mushrooms
- 1/2 cup alkaline barbecue sauce
- 1/4 cup spring water
- 1 tsp. Sea salt
- 1 tsp. Powdered onion
- 1/2 tsp. cayenne
- Grapeseed oil
- Basting brush
- Cast-iron griddle
- Skewers (optional)

**Directions**

1. Scrape gills off each mushroom cap's underside to prevent an earthy flavor, then slice mushrooms about 1/2 inch apart. Add mushrooms to a wide pot then add seasonings, water, then barbecue sauce for the most part.
2. Cover with a lid, shake and keep for around 6-8 hours in the refrigerator. Flip the container after 2 hours. Take a skewer and pass around the center by 3 mushrooms, add the other skewer, then attach another 2-3 more pieces. You should cook these as riblets if some slices fall.
3. This dish may also be served on a grill, cooked in a skillet or cooked at 350 degrees F for 10-15 minutes (after step 4). You can also cook the mushrooms like riblets, if you don't have skewers.
4. Spray the griddle with oil over medium heat and cook the ribs for 12-15 minutes, tossing after 3 minutes. Brush with more barbecue sauce, if a few more flips are desired.

**Nutrition**: 119 calories16g fiber32g protein6g sugar

# Alkaline Electric Sloppy Joe

**Preparation Time**: 10 minutes

**Cooking Time**: 30 minutes

**Servings**: 4-6

**Ingredients**

- 2 cups of cooked spelt or kamut

- 1 cup of cooked garbanzo beans
- 1 1/2 cup of Alkaline Barbecue sauce
- 1/2 cup of onion
- 1/2 cup of green peppers
- 1 cup of plum tomato,
- 1 tsp. Powder of onion
- 1 tsp. of sea salt
- 1/8 tsp. Cayenne powder
- Grapeseed oil

**Directions**

1. In food processor, put the spelt and garbanzo beans and process for around 10-15 seconds. Add oil and sauté onions, peppers, and seasonings in a large skillet over medium-high heat for 3-5 minutes.
2. Mix sauce with pulsed **ingredients**, tomato, and barbecue and cook for about 5 minutes. Serve on Alkaline Flatbread and enjoy!

**Nutrition**: 215 calories36g protein20g fiber9g sugar

# Alkaline Electric Flatbread

**Preparation Time**: 10 minutes

**Cooking Time**: 20 minutes

**Servings**: 4 - 6

**Ingredients**

- 2 cups Flour spelt
- 2 tbsp. Grapeseed oil
- 3/4 cup Spring Water
- 1 tbsp. Sea salt
- 2 tsp. Oregano
- 2 tsp. Basil
- 2 tsp. Powdered onion
- 1/4 tsp. Cayenne

**Directions**

1. Mix flour and seasonings together, until well blended. In the mixture, add in oil and around 1/2 cup of water. Mix in water gradually, until it turns into a ball. Add the flour to the workspace and knead the dough for around 5 minutes, then split it into 6 equal portions.
2. Roll out each ball into circles measuring about 4 inches. Put it on medium-high heat in an ungreased skillet, tossing until ready every 2-3 minutes. Enjoy your Alkaline Flatbread!

**Nutrition**: 115 calories31g protein24g fiber5g sugar

# Alkaline Electric Meatloaf

**Preparation Time**: 12 minutes

**Cooking Time**: 25 minutes

**Servings**: 6

**Ingredients**

- 3 cups Mushrooms, sliced
- 2 cups Cooked Garbanzo Beans
- 2/3 cup Alkaline Barbecue Sauce or Alkaline Ketchup
- 1 1/2 cup Garbanzo Bean Flour
- 1 cup White Onions, chopped
- 1 cup Green Peppers, chopped
- 1 Roma tomato, chopped
- 1 tsp. Agave
- 2 tbsp. Onion powder
- 1 tbsp. Sea salt
- 1 tbsp. Basil
- 1 tsp. Oregano
- 2 tsp. Savory
- 1 tsp. powdered ginger
- 1/2 tsp. Cayenne Powder

**Directions**

1. Blend mushrooms and garbanzo beans together for 30 seconds in food processor. Process for 1 minute or until fully blended in seasonings, agave, 1/2 cup of white onions, 1/2 cup of green peppers and 1/3 cup barbecue sauce.
2. In a large bowl, add the mixture and mix in 1/3 cup of onions, 1/3 cup of peppers and 1 cup of flour. If the mixture is too moist put more flour. Bake in oven for 35-45 minutes at 350 F.
3. Allow at least 30 minutes to cool before cutting into meatloaf or it may be mushy and fall apart. Enjoy your Electric Alkaline meatloaf

**Nutrition**: 207 calories37g protein8g fiber5g sugar

# Alkaline Electric Burro Mashed "Potatoes"

**Preparation Time**: 5 minutes

**Cooking time**: 35 minutes

**Servings**: 4-6

**Ingredients**:

- 6-8 Green Burro Bananas * or 2 cups Cooked Garbanzo Beans
- 1 cup Hemp Milk or Walnut Milk
- 2 tsp. Powder onion
- 2 tsp. Sea Salt
- 1/4 cup Green Onions, diced with Alkaline Gravy (Optional)

**Directions**:

1.  Split off the ends of each burro, cut each side through the skin,  extract the flesh and add to the processor. Pour the milk and seasonings into the food processor and blend for 1-2 minutes, then add spring water if the mixture becomes too thick.
2.  Add mixture and green onions to a pan, and cook over medium heat. Cook while stirring continuously for 25-30 minutes, adding more water when it becomes too dense. Serve, with Alkaline Gravy!

**Nutrition**: 157 calories50g protein20g fiber4g sugar

# Alkaline Electric Mushroom & Onion Gravy

**Preparation Time**: 8 minutes

**Cooking Time**: 25 minutes

**Servings**: 2-3

**Ingredients**:

-   2 - 3 cups Spring Water
-   1/2 cup Mushrooms (optional)
-   1/2 cup Onions
-   1/4 tsp. Cayenne
-   3 tbs. Garbanzo bean flour
-   2 tbs. Grapeseed Oil
-   1 tsp. Sea Salt
-   1/2 tsp. Thyme
-   1 tsp. Onion Powder
-   1/2 tsp. Oregano

**Directions**:

1.  Add grapeseed oil over medium to high heat to fry pan. Sauté mushrooms & onions for A minute. Add all seasonings and spices except cayenne. Sautee for Five minutes. Add 2 cups of spring water. Add ground cayenne. Mix all **ingredients** completely and bring to a boil. Continue sifting a little at a time the flour, and mix with a whisk to avoid lumps. Start cooking until boiling, including remaining water if needed

**Nutrition**: 116 calories16g fiber32g protein7g sugar

# Alkaline Electric Spicy Kale

**Preparation Time**: 5 minutes

**Cooking Time**: 15 minutes

**Servings**: 4

**Ingredients**:

- 1 bunch of Kale
- 1/4 cup Onion, diced
- 1/4 cup Red Pepper, diced
- 1 tsp. Crushed Red Pepper
- 1/4 tsp. Sea Salt
- Alkaline "Garlic" Oil or Grape Seed Oil

**Directions**:

1. Rinse off the kale, then fold in half per leaf, then cut off the base. Air dry the kale.
2. Chop the kale into bite-sized bits and use salad spinner to drain water. Add approx. 2 tbsp. Oil to wok over high heat. Stir in onions and peppers for 2-3 minutes.
3. Reduce heat to low, add the kale to the wok and cover for 5 minutes with a lid. Add crushed red pepper, mix and cover with lid for an additional 3 minutes or until tender.

**Nutrition**: 104 calories15g fiber25g protein8g sugar

# Veggie Kabobs

**Preparation Time**: 20 minutes

**Cooking Time**: 10 minutes

Serves: 4

**Ingredients**:

- For Marinade
- 2 garlic cloves, minced
- 2 teaspoons fresh basil, minced
- 2 teaspoons fresh oregano, minced
- ½ teaspoon cayenne powder
- Sea salt, as required
- 2 tablespoons fresh key lime juice
- 2 tablespoons avocado oil
- For Veggies
- 2 large zucchinis, cut into thick slices
- 8 large button mushrooms, quartered
- 1 yellow bell pepper, seeded and cubed
- 1 red bell pepper, seeded and cubed

**Directions**:

1. For marinade:
2. Mix all the **ingredients** in a bowl. Mix in the vegetables and toss it well for evenly coat. Cover and refrigerate to marinate for at least 6-8 hours.

3. Preheat the grill to medium-high heat. Generously, grease the grill grate. Remove the vegetables from the bowl and thread onto pre-soaked wooden skewers.  Grill for about 8-10 minutes or until done completely, flipping occasionally.

**Nutrition**: 122 Calories7.8g Total Fat4.3g Protein12.7g Carbs3.5g Fiber

# Spiced Okra

**Preparation Time**: 10 minutes

**Cooking Time**: 13 minutes

**Serving**: 2

**Ingredients**:

- 1 tablespoon avocado oil
- ¾ pound okra pods, 2-inch pieces
- ½ teaspoon ground cumin
- ½ teaspoon cayenne powder
- Sea salt, as required

**Directions**:

1. Cook the oil over medium heat and stir fry the okra for about 2 minutes. Reduce the heat to low and cook covered for about 6-8 minutes stirring occasionally. Add the cumin, cayenne powder and salt and stir to combine. Increase the heat to medium and cook uncovered for about 2-3 minutes more. Remove from the heat and serve hot.

**Nutrition**: 81 Calories1.4g Total Fat3.5g Protein13.5g Carbs5.9g Fiber

# Mushroom Curry

**Preparation Time**: 15 minutes

**Cooking Time**: 25 minutes

**Serving**: 4

**Ingredients**:

- 2 cups plum tomatoes, chopped
- 2 tablespoons grapeseed oil
- 1 small onion, chopped finely
- ¼ teaspoon cayenne powder
- 4 cups fresh button mushrooms, sliced
- 1¼ cups spring water
- ¼ cup unsweetened coconut milk
- Sea salt, as required

**Directions**:

1. In a food processor, add the tomatoes and pulse until a smooth paste form. In a pan, heat the oil over medium heat and sauté the onion for about 5-6 minutes. Add the tomato paste and cook for about 5 minutes. Stir in the mushrooms, water and coconut milk and bring to a boil. Cook for about 10-12 minutes, stirring occasionally. Season it well and remove from the heat. Serve hot.

**Nutrition**: 126 Calories9.5g Total Fat3.7g Protein9g Carbs2.1g Fiber

# Bell Peppers & Zucchini Stir Fry

**Preparation Time**: 15 minutes

**Cooking Time**: 15 minutes

**Servings**: 4

**Ingredients**:

- 2 tablespoons avocado oil
- 1 large onion, cubed
- 4 garlic cloves, minced
- 1 large green bell pepper
- 1 large red bell pepper
- 1 large yellow bell pepper
- 2 cups zucchini, sliced
- ¼ cup spring water
- Sea salt, as required
- Cayenne powder, as required

**Directions**:

1. Cook the oil over medium heat and sauté the onion and garlic for about 4-5 minutes. Add the vegetables and stir fry for about 4-5 minutes. Add the water and stir fry for about 3-4 minutes more. Serve hot.

**Nutrition**: 66 Calories1.3g Total Fat2.3g Protein13.5g Carbs3g Fiber

# Barred Zucchini Hummus Wrap

**Preparation Time**: 15 minutes

**Cooking Time**: 10 minutes

**Servings**: 4

**Ingredients**

- ½ of medium red onion; peeled, sliced
- 2 medium plum tomato, sliced
- 2 cups romaine lettuce, chopped
- 2 large zucchinis
- ½ teaspoon sea salt

- ½ teaspoon cayenne pepper
- 2 tablespoons grapeseed oil
- 4 spelt flour tortillas
- 8 tablespoons hummus, homemade

**Directions**

1. Rinse the zucchinis, cut their ends, and then cut into slices. Take a grill pan, place it over medium heat, grease the pan generously with oil, and let it heat. Meanwhile, take a medium bowl, place zucchini slices in it, season with salt and cayenne pepper, pour in the oil, and then toss until well coated.
2. Spread the zucchini slices onto the heated grill pan, cook for 3 minutes until golden-brown, then turn the zucchini slices and continue cooking for another 2 minutes. Set aside until needed.
3. Heat the tortillas: place them onto the grill pan and then cook for 1 minute per side until hot and grill marks appear on the bread.
4. Assemble the wraps: working on one wrap at a time, spread 2 tablespoons of hummus on one side of a tortilla, spread one-fourth of the zucchini slices, and then top with ½ cup lettuce and one-fourth of the tomato slices. Wrap tightly, repeat with the remaining tortillas, and then serve

**Nutrition**: 270 Calories32g Carbs21g Fat17g Protein

# Vegetable Tacos

**Preparation Time**: 10 minutes

**Cooking Time**: 12 minutes

**Servings**: 4

**Ingredients**

- 4 large Portobello mushrooms
- 2 medium red bell peppers; cored, sliced
- 4 medium green bell peppers; cored, sliced
- 2 medium white onion; peeled, sliced
- 2/3 teaspoon onion powder
- 2/3 teaspoon habanero seasoning
- 2/3 teaspoon cayenne pepper
- 1 key lime, juiced
- 2 tablespoons grapeseed oil
- 2 medium avocados; peeled, pitted, sliced
- 8 tortillas, corn-free

**Directions**

1. Prepare the mushrooms: remove their stems and gills, rinse them well, and then slice mushrooms into 1/3-inch-thick pieces.

2. Take a large skillet pan, place it over medium heat, add 1 tablespoon oil and when hot, add onion and bell pepper and then cook for 2 minutes until tender-crisp.
3. Add sliced mushrooms, sprinkle with all the seasoning, stir until coated, and then continue cooking for 7–8 minutes until vegetables have softened.
4. Meanwhile, heat the tortillas until warm.
5. Assemble the tacos: spoon the cooked fajitas evenly into the center of each tortilla, top with avocado, and drizzle with lime juice.
6. Serve straight away.

**Nutrition**: 414.7 Calories73.3g Carbs7.4g Fat19.4g Protein

# Spicy Kale

**Preparation Time**: 5 minutes

**Cooking Time**: 15 minutes

**Servings**: 4

**Ingredients**

- ¼ cup white onion, diced
- 1 bunch of kale, fresh
- ¼ cup red pepper, diced
- ¼ teaspoon sea salt
- 1 teaspoon crushed red pepper
- 2 tablespoons grapeseed oil

**Directions**

1. Prepare the kale: rinse it well, remove its stem, and then cut the leaves into bite-size pieces. Drain well by using a salad spinner.
2. Take a large skillet pan, place it over high heat, add oil and when hot, add onion and red pepper, season with salt, and then cook for 3 minutes or until beginning to tender.
3. Switch heat to low, add kale leaves into the pan, stir until mixed, then cover the pan with a lid and continue cooking for 5 minutes.
4. Sprinkle red pepper over kale, toss until mixed, return lid over the pan, and cook for another 3 minutes until vegetables have become tender. Serve straight away.

**Nutrition**: 155 Calories34.7g Carbs65.3g Fat

# Zucchini Noodles with Avocado Sauce

**Preparation Time**: 10 minutes

**Cooking Time**: 20 minutes

**Servings**: 4

**Ingredients**

- 4 large zucchinis, destemmed
- 4 avocados; pitted, peeled, sliced
- 4 cups basil leaves
- 48 cherry tomatoes, sliced
- 1 ½ teaspoon salt
- 1 cup walnuts, chopped
- 8 tablespoons key lime juice
- 1 cup of water

**Directions**

1. Prepare zucchini: remove the ends of each zucchini and then make noodles by using a spiralizer or vegetable peeler. Set aside until needed.
2. Place avocado into a blender, add basil, salt, and nuts, pour in lime juice and water, and then pulse at high speed for 1–2 minutes until smooth sauce comes together.
3. Transfer zucchini noodles into a large bowl, pour in the blended sauce, add tomatoes, and then toss until well combined and noodles are coated with the sauce.  Serve straight away.

**Nutrition**: 240 Calories10g Carbs22g Fat3g Protein

# Enoki Mushroom Pasta

**Preparation Time**: 25 minutes

**Cooking Time**: 1 hour

**Servings**: 4

**Ingredients**

- 2 packs of enoki mushrooms, about 400 grams total
- 8 round slices of butternut squash, fresh
- 3 medium white onions; peeled, sliced
- 4 medium bell peppers; cored, sliced
- 2 cups cherry tomatoes
- 1 ½ teaspoons sea salt
- 4 tablespoons coconut oil

**Directions**

1. Prepare the squash: cut the squash into eight slices, peel them, and then remove seeds. Take a large pot half full with water, place it over medium-high heat, bring it to a boil, and then add butternut squash.
2. Cook squash for 30 to 45 minutes until tender, pour out the excess cooking liquid, and then mash by using a fork. Add onion, bell pepper, and mushrooms into the pot and then let it simmer for 15–20 minutes until tender.
3. Season with salt, then remove the pot from heat and let the mixture cool for 15 minutes. Add coconut oil, wait until it melts, and then stir well. Divide pasta evenly among four plates, top with cherry tomatoes, and then serve.

**Nutrition**: 669.5 Calories88.3g Carbs29.8g Fat11.7g Protein

# Tuna Bites

**Preparation Time**: 15 minutes

**Cooking Time**: 0 minute

**Servings**: 4

**Ingredients**

- 2/3 sheet of nori
- 2 cups walnuts, chopped
- 4 key limes, juiced
- 2 Roma tomatoes
- ¼ teaspoon onion powder
- ¼ teaspoon dried oregano
- ¼ teaspoon ginger powder
- ¼ teaspoon dried thyme
- ¼ teaspoon sea salt
- ¼ teaspoon cayenne powder
- 2 tablespoons coconut oil

**Directions**

1. Prepare the nori sheets: fold it into three equal folds and then cut along the first crease to remove one-third of the nori sheet.
2. Now fold the cut one-third of nori sheet in half, cut along the crease, lay these pieces on top of each other, fold them in half, and then cut along the crease.
3. Repeat with the remaining nori sheet and place the pieces into a food processor.
4. Prepare the tomatoes: cut off the tops, and then cut each tomato into five equal pieces.
5. Add tomatoes into the food processor, add remaining **ingredients**, cover with the lid, and then pulse for 3–4 minutes until well mixed and thoroughly blended.
6. Shape the mixture into rough balls, transfer them to a plate, and then serve.

**Nutrition**: 474.8 Calories14.2g Carbs42.7g Fat8.3g Protein

# Juicy Portobello Burgers

**Preparation Time**: 15 minutes

**Cooking Time**: 20 minutes

**Servings**: 4

**Ingredients**

- 4 large Portobello mushroom caps
- 2 large avocados; pitted, peeled, flesh sliced
- 2 medium tomato, sliced

- 2 cups purslane
- Marinade
- 2 teaspoons cayenne pepper
- 4 teaspoons dried basil
- 2 teaspoons dried oregano
- 1 teaspoon onion powder
- 6 tablespoons olive oil

## Directions

1. Prepare the mushrooms: slice it like a bun by removing the stem from each mushroom and then slice off ½-inch of the top.  Prepare the marinade: take a small bowl, place all of its **ingredients** in it, and then whisk until well combined.
2. Take a cookie sheet, line it with foil, grease it with oil, and then place the prepared mushroom caps on it. Pour the prepared marinade into each mushroom cap and then let it rest for 10 minutes.
3. Meanwhile, preheat the oven to 425ºF. After 10 minutes, place the mushroom caps into the oven and then bake for 10 minutes per side until tender. When done, distribute baked mushroom caps among plates, cap-side up, and then stuff evenly with avocado, tomato, and purslane.
4. Serve straight away.

**Nutrition**: 324 Calories8.9g Carbs30.6g Fat4.1g Protein

# Chinese Cucumber Salad Magnifico

**Preparation Time**: 15 minutes

**Cooking Time**: 0 minute

**Serving**: 4

**Ingredients**

- 1 pound of fresh cucumber
- 4 cloves of garlic
- 3 tablespoon of sesame seed oil
- Just a pinch of salt
- Pinch of pepper

**Directions**:

1. Take a bowl and add oil. Add salt and just a pinch of pepper. Add minced up garlic to the bowl and toss them well to mix everything up
2. Wash the cucumbers well and cut them in half
3. Cut the halves into slices
4. Add the slices to the bowl and toss them well to ensure that they are coated well
5. Chill the salad in your fridge for 10 minutes

**Nutrition**: 20 Calories4g Carbs1g Fiber

# Buckwheat Pasta mixed up with Bell Pepper and  Broccoli

**Preparation Time**: 5 minutes

**Cooking Time**: 10 minutes

**Serving**: 3-4

**Ingredients**

- 500g of buckwheat pasta
- 4 tablespoon of extra virgin olive oil cold pressed out
- 2 diced up cloves of garlic
- 1 middle sized white onion ring
- Strips of 1 red bell pepper
- 1 big broccoli head cut up into florets
- 3 diced up middle sized tomatoes
- 3 sliced up carrots
- 1 tablespoon of fresh lemon juice
- 1 teaspoon of oregano
- 1 teaspoon of yeast free vegetable broth
- Sea salt as needed
- Pepper as needed

**Directions**

1. The vegetables into bite sized portions. Take a pot of water and add salt. Heat it up and buckwheat pasta. Cook it to Al Dente
2. Take another pot and add broccoli and water. Cook these as well. Take a pan and place it over medium heat. Add 2 tablespoon of olive oil and add onions and garlic
3. Sauté them. Take out and keep it on the side
4. Add 2 tablespoon of oil to the pan and cook veggies until tender
5. Make sure to first cook the carrots, then bell pepper and finally tomatoes
6. Drain the cooked broccoli and add the broccoli and onions to the pan with vegetables
7. Add lemon juice, oregano, and vegetable broth
8. Season with salt and pepper to adjust the flavor. Stir well
9. Add the veggie mix over your buckwheat pasta and serve!

**Nutrition**: 583 Calories26g Fats61g Carbs4g Fiber

# Mix-Mix Alkaline Veggie

**Preparation Time**: 5 minutes

**Cooking Time**: 10 minutes

**Serving**: 2

**Ingredients**:

- 15 kale leaves (chopped)
- 1 cup of watercress leaves
- 1 cucumber (diced)
- 2 tbsp. fresh dill (finely chopped)
- ¼ red onion (chopped)
- 5-10 sliced olives
- ¼ red bell pepper (chopped)
- ¼ green bell pepper (chopped)
- 1 tbsp. 100% date sugar syrup
- 3 tbsp. water
- ⅛ tsp of sea salt

**Directions**:

1. Mix the date sugar syrup, water, and salt together. Stir in the remaining **ingredients** together in a bowl. Massage in date syrup mix with the vegetables. Toss and serve.

**Nutrition**: 102 calories5.8g fiber11g protein

# Nori Wraps with Fresh Vegetables and Quinoa

**Preparation Time**: 15 minutes

**Cooking Time**: 20 minutes

**Serving**: 1

**Ingredients**:

- 2 Nori sheets
- ¼ cup Raw carrot sticks
- ½ cup Cooked quinoa
- ¼ cup Raw carrot sticks
- 1tsp Fresh garlic, finely chopped
- 1bsp Raw seed mix
- 1tsp Fresh ginger root, finely grated
- ¼ cup Raw cucumber sticks
- ¼ cup Fresh coriander leaves, finely chopped
- 1 tbsp Sesame oilseed

**Directions**:

1. Get a bowl and mix cooked quinoa with coriander leaves, ginger, seed mix, coriander leaves, and garlic.

2. Pour the sesame oil seed and mix properly. Spread out both nori sheets on two surfaces. Spread the quinoa mix one each nori sheets. Add carrot sticks and cucumber on top of the quinoa.
3. Fold up the nori sheets with the quinoa **ingredients** inside. Depending on how you like it, serve with pickled ginger or soy sauce.

**Nutrition**: 205 calories15g fiber26g protein

# Kale Wraps with Chili, Garlic, Cucumber, Coriander, and Green Beans

**Preparation Time**: 30 minutes

**Cooking Time**: 20 minutes

**Servings**: 1

**Ingredients**:

- 1 tbsp Fresh lime juice
- 1 tbsp Raw seed mix
- 2 Kale leaves
- 2 tsp Fresh garlic
- ½ Ripe avocado
- 1 tsp Fresh red chili
- 1 cup Fresh cucumber sticks
- ½ cup Fresh coriander leaves
- 1 cup Green beans

**Directions**:

1. Spread kale leaves on a clean kitchen work surface. Spread each chopped coriander leaves on each leaf, position them around the end of the leaf, perpendicular to the edge.
2. Spread green beans equally on each leaf, at the edge of each leaf, same as the coriander leaves. Do the same thing with the cucumber sticks.
3. Cut the divide chopped garlic across each leaf, sprinkling it all over the green beans. Cut and share the chopped chili across each leaf and sprinkle it over the garlic. Now, divide the avocado across each leaf, and spread it over chili, garlic, coriander and green beans.
4. Share the raw seed mix among each leaf, and sprinkle them over other **ingredients**. Divide the lime juice on across each leaf and drizzle it over all other **ingredients**.
5. Now fold or roll up the kale leaves and wrap up all the **ingredients** within it. You can serve with soy sauce!

**Nutrition**: 305 calories18g fiber30g protein

# Cabbage Wraps with Avocado, Asparagus, Pecan Nuts and Strawberries

**Preparation Time**: 30 minutes

**Cooking Time**: 15 minutes

**Serving**: 1

**Ingredients**:

- ½ cup Raw pecan nuts
- ½ cup Fresh sliced strawberries
- 2 Cabbage leaves
- ½ Ripe avocado
- 1 cup Green asparagus spears

**Directions**:

1. Spread out the cabbage sheets on a clean kitchen work surface. Share the asparagus shear among each cabbage leaf and place them on the edge of the leaf. Share the avocado slices on each leaf and put them on top of the asparagus spears.
2. Share the strawberries over each leaf and spread on top of the avocado slices. Share the pecan nuts between each leaf and spread it on the strawberries.
3. Wrap the leaves with all **ingredients** inside them. Serve with soy sauce (optional).

**Nutrition**: 119 calories13g fiber31g protein

# Millet Tabbouleh, Lime and Cilantro

**Preparation Time**: 10 minutes

**Cooking Time**: 30 minutes

**Servings**: 6

**Ingredients**:

- ½ cup Lime juice
- ½ cup Cilantro
- 6 drops Hot sauce
- ¼ cup and 2tsp Olive oil
- 2 Tomatoes
- 2 Green onions
- 2 Cucumber
- 1 cup Millet

**Directions**:

1. Heat olive oil in a saucepan over medium heat. Add the millet and fry until it begins to smell fragrant (this takes between three (3) to four (4) minutes). Add about six (6) cups of water and bring to boil.
2. Wait for about fifteen (15) minutes. Turn off the heat, wash and rinse under cold water. Drain the millet and transfer to a large bowl.

3.  Add cucumbers, tomatoes, lime juice, cilantro, green onions, the ¼ cup oil, and hot sauce. Season with pepper and salt to taste.

**Nutrition**: 211 calories15g fiber30g protein

# Alkaline Cauliflower Fried Rice with Kale, Ginger, And Turmeric

**Preparation Time**: 5 minutes

**Cooking Time**: 5 minutes

**Servings**: 4

**Ingredients**:

- 1 Lime
- 4 Spring onions
- 2 Almonds
- 1 tbsp Coconut oil
- 1 Cauliflower (large
- 1 bunch Mint
- inch Fresh root turmeric
- 1 Zucchini (courgette)
- ½ bunch Kale
- 1 Cauliflower
- 1 tsp Tamari soy sauce
- ½ bunch Parsley

**Directions**:

1.  First of all, cut the cauliflower into smaller florets and blend in a food processor or blender. Process until it begins to look like rice. Next, prep the veggies. Roughly chop off the herbs like parsley, mint, and  coriander.
2.  Throw away the parsley and mint stems but keep that off the coriander. Slice the courgette and kale thinly. Peel off the turmeric and ginger, then grate both into a pan containing coconut oil. Once it begins to get warm, stir the mint, parsley and coriander and coriander stem into the mix.
3.  Wait for thirty seconds and stir in the kale and cauliflower. After two to three minutes, add the tamari, spring onions and the remaining herbs. Stir properly and turn off the heat.
4.  Lastly, chop the almonds, stir through. Season to taste and sprinkle lime.

**Nutrition**: 304 calories14g fiber33g protein

# Alkaline Salad with Mint and Lemon Toppings

**Preparation Time**: 15 minutes

**Cooking Time**: 20 minutes

**Servings**: 4

**Ingredients**:

- 200g Green peas
- 5 Radish
- ½ bunch Cilantro
- Avocado (sliced)
- 3 Asparagus
- ½ bunch Flat leaf parsley
- 2 Courgette (zucchini)

**For the dressing:**

- 2 Shallots
- 3 Lemons
- 15g Dijon Mustard
- 1 Garlic clove
- 190ml Olive oil
- Black pepper and Himalayan salt to taste
- ¼ bunch Mint

**Directions**:

1. First of all, let's start with the asparagus. Boil water in a pan, when it gets to the boiling point, immerse the asparagus inside, for about one minute.
2. Remove it and rinse immediately in cold water. After that, slice it in long strips. Next, get a frying pan and fry the Zucchini over medium heat until it begins to turn brown.
3. Get a large bowl, mix the cilantro, radish, parsley, peas, avocado, asparagus and zucchini. In other to make the dressing, blend all **ingredients** in a food processor. Finally, dress and season.

**Nutrition**: 258 calories17g fiber28g protein

# Alkaline Sushi-Roll Ups

**Preparation Time**: 15 minutes

**Cooking Time**: 20 minutes

**Servings**: 2

**Ingredients**:

**For hummus**

- 1 Clove of garlic
- ½ Lemon juice
- Almonds handful
- 1 pinch Cumin

- 1 pinch Himalayan salt
- A glug Olive oil
- 1 tsp Tahini
- 100g Chickpeas

**For the roll-ups:**

- 1 Cucumber
- 2 Zucchini/Courgette
- 1 Carrot
- 1 Capsicum
- 1 small Coriander/cilantro
- 1 Avocado

**Directions**:

1. For the Hummus
2. All you have to do is to get a food processor or blender. Blend until everything is smooth.
3. Then add some more lemon or olive oil to suit your taste.
4. For the Alkaline Sushi Roll-Ups
5. Cut off both ends of the Zucchini Use a vegetable peeler to peel it into thin, long strips
6. Lay out the zucchini strip and spread the almond hummus on it
7. Add some matchsticks of avocado, veggies and a few pieces of coriander. Spray some of the sesame seeds on top. Roll and enjoy

**Nutrition**: 158 calories10g fiber9g fats

# Artichoke Sauce Ala Quinoa Pasta

**Preparation Time**: 15 minutes

**Cooking Time**: 0 minute

**Serving**: 4

**Ingredients**

- 7 ounce or 200g spelled pasta
- 8 ounce or 220g of frozen artichoke
- 5 ounces of fresh tomatoes
- 1 medium sized onion
- 1 clove of garlic
- 1 ounce of pine nuts
- 1 teaspoon of yeast free vegetable stock
- 3 tablespoons of fresh basil
- ½ a teaspoon of yeast free vegetable stock
- 3 tablespoons of fresh basil
- ½ a teaspoon of organic sea salt
- 1 pinch of cayenne pepper
- 2 tablespoon of cold pressed extra virgin olive oil

**Directions**

1.  Prepare your Artichokes by cooking them gently until they show a tender texture
2.  Cook the pasta to Al Dente following the instructions on your packet
3.  Take out your tomatoes and cut them up into cubes
4.  Chop up the onions, garlic, and basil into bite sized portions
5.  Take a pan and add 2 tablespoons of olive oil over medium heat
6.  Add pine nuts, garlic, and onion and stir them for a few minutes
7.  Take another bowl and add ½ a cup of water and dissolve yeast free veggie stock
8.  Add the mixture to the pan. Simmer it over low heat and keep stirring it for 2 minutes
9.  Once done, add basil and season with cayenne pepper and salt
10. Pour the sauce over your pasta. Serve!

**Nutrition**: 286 Calories13g Fats26g Carbs3g Fiber

# Special Pasta Ala Pepper and Tomato Sauce

**Preparation Time**: 5 minutes

**Cooking Time**: 10 minutes

**Serving**: 4

**Ingredients**

- 500g of vegetable pasta
- 300g of tomatoes
- ½ a cup of sun-dried tomatoes
- 1 small sized red bell pepper
- 1 small sized Zucchini
- 1 piece of onion
- 2 pieces of garlic cloves
- 1 piece of chili
- 5 pieces of fresh basil leaves
- 2-3 tablespoon of cold pressed olive oil
- Sea salt as needed
- Pepper as needed

**Directions**

1.  Cook the pasta properly according to the specified package instructions. Cut up the tomatoes, bell pepper, zucchini into fine cubes and chop the chili, garlic, and onions. Take a pan and place it over medium heat
2.  Add oil and heat up the oil. Add onions, chili, pepper, and garlic and fry them for a few minutes
3.  Add tomatoes, zucchini and cook for 5-10 minutes more. Add basil
4.  Season with pepper and salt to adjust the flavor

5.  Add pasta on top your **serving** plate
6.  Pour the sauce and season Serve!

**Nutrition:** 591 Calories22g Fats73g Carbs

# Southern Amazing Salad

**Preparation Time**: 15 minutes

**Cooking Time**: 0 minute

**Serving**: 2

**Ingredients**

- 5 cups of Romaine lettuce
- ½ a cup of sprouted black beans
- 1 cup of halved cherry tomatoes
- 1 diced avocado
- ¼ cup of chopped almonds
- ½ cup of fresh cilantro
- ½ a cup of Salsa Fresca

**Directions**

1.  Take a large sized bowl and add lettuce, tomatoes, beans, almonds, cilantro, avocado, Salsa
    Fresco. Toss everything well and mix them. Divide the salad into **serving** bowls and serve!

**Nutrition**370 Calories16g Fats44g Carbs14g Fiber

# A Concoction of Roast Veggies

**Preparation Time**: 10 minutes

**Cooking Time**: 15 minutes

**Serving**: 2

**Ingredients**

- ½ a bunch of trimmed asparagus
- 1 pint of cherry tomatoes
- ½ a cup of halved mushrooms
- 1 peeled carrot cut up into bite sized portions
- 1 red bell pepper
- 1 yellow bell pepper (both peppers should be deseeded and cut into bite sized portions)
- 1 tablespoon of coconut oil
- 1 tablespoon of garlic powder
- 1 teaspoon of sea salt

**Directions**

1.  Preheat your oven to a temperature of 425 degrees Fahrenheit

2. Take a bowl and add asparagus, mushrooms, tomatoes, bell pepper and carrot
3. Add coconut milk, salt, garlic powder and toss everything well to ensure that everything mixed
4. Transfer the mixed veggies to a baking pan and place the pan in a pre-heated oven
5. Roast for 15 minutes until they are nice and tender
6. Transfer the roasted veggies to a bowl
7. Divide into **serving** bowls and enjoy!

**Nutrition**132 Calories7.3g Fats15g Carbs5g Fiber

# Pad Thai

**Preparation Time**: 10 minutes

**Cooking Time**: 0 minute

**Serving**: 2

**Ingredients**

- 4 cups of chopped iceberg lettuce
- 1 cup of bean sprouts
- 2 carrots cut up into thin slices
- 1 piece of zucchini cut up into strips
- 1 finely chopped scallion
- 2 tablespoons of chopped almonds
- 1 lime juice
- 1 clove of garlic
- 1 teaspoon of tamarind paste
- 1 pack of stevia
- ½ a teaspoon of sea salt

**Directions**

1. Take a large sized bowl and add lettuce carrots, zucchini, bean sprouts and almonds
2. Take a small sized food processor bowl and add garlic, lime juice, stevia, salt, and blend well
3. Pour the dressing over your veggies and mix well
4. Divide the mixture into **serving** bowl and enjoy!

**Nutrition**77 Calories3.2g Fats6.4g Carbs5.5g Fiber

# The Mysterious Alkaline Veggies and Rice

**Preparation Time**: 10 minutes

**Cooking Time**: 5 minutes

**Serving**: 4

**Ingredients**

- 1 cup of wild rice

- 1 cup of Pak Choi
- 1 cup o Broccoli
- 1 cup of Young Beans
- 2 cups of Carrots
- 1 cup of bean sprout
- ½ a cup of vegetable broth
- 1 piece of chili
- 1 fresh juice of lime
- Cilantro as needed
- Basil as required
- Seas Salt as required

**Directions**

1. Chop up the Pak Choi, carrots, beans, bean sprouts, and broccoli
2. Add them to a pan and pour vegetable broth
3. Steam fry the mixture until they are fully cooked and are a bit crunchy
4. Take a mortar and pestle and add cilantro and chopped up chili
5. Pour lime juice and mix well to prepare the dressing
6. Take a **serving** platter add rice, add the prepped vegetables
7. Serve by pouring the dressing over them!

**Nutrition**: 200 Calories2g Fats33g Carbs2g Fiber

# Tomato and Garlic Soup

**Preparation Time**: 40 minutes

**Cooking Time**: 20 minutes

**Servings**: 2

**Ingredients**:

- ½ liter of water
- 1 purple onion
- 8-10 cloves of garlic rolled
- 1 kilo of ripe tomatoes, without skin
- 2 or 3 bay leaves
- 1 pinch of cayenne pepper
- 1 pinch of black pepper
- Sea salt, to taste
- 1 tsp. Provencal herbs
- 1 pinch of cumin to it sprinkle
- Extra virgin olive oil

**Directions**:

1. In a pot, sauté the onion and garlic in 1 tablespoon of olive oil. Remove often, so they do not burn. Blanch the tomatoes into boiling water, remove the skin and, if you prefer, also the seeds.
2. Add to the pot the tomatoes cut in quarters and the rest of the **ingredients**. Remove and cook over low heat for 10 minutes and with the pot covered, until the tomato acquires a slightly orange tone.
3. Add the water, and boil for about 10 minutes. Remove the bay leaves and crush until you get a light texture. If necessary, add more water and rectify salt.
4. Serve the hot soup dressed with a strand of extra virgin olive oil and sprinkled with the cumin. To learn more: "Help fight infections with the antibiotic power of garlic," explains **nutrition**ist Llargués. It has traditionally been used to prevent infections. Its flavor is dominant, compensated in this recipe by the tomato.

**Nutrition**: 81.3 Calories2.1g Total Fat2.7g Dietary Fiber31g protein

# Kale Soup

**Preparation Time**: 10 minutes

**Cooking Time**: 30 minutes

**Servings**: 2

**Ingredients**

- 2 tablespoons olive oil
- 1/2 piece white onion filleted
- 1 celery stick cut in cubes
- 1 cup chopped pore
- 1 tablespoon finely chopped garlic
- 1 cup sliced mushrooms
- 1 cup mushroom filleted
- 2 cups of kale
- 1/2 piece of fennel the bulb into sticks
- 6 cups of beef broth
- 1 pinch of salt
- 1 pinch of pepper
- 1/4 cup of almond

**Directions**:

1. Heat a medium deep pot over medium heat, add the olive oil, onion and celery until they release the aroma, add the pore, garlic and mushrooms with the mushrooms until they start to release the juice, add the kale until I soften with the fennel. Cook for 5 more minutes.
2. Fill with the beef broth and season to your liking. Cook until it boils, covering it to prevent it from evaporating. Serve in a bowl with a little fresh kale at the end and sliced almonds. Enjoy

**Nutrition**: 507 Calories65.6g Carbohydrates35.8g Proteins11.9g Dietary fiber10.7g Sugars

# Pumpkin Cream

**Preparation Time**: 25 minutes

**Cooking Time**: 45 minutes

**Servings**: 1

**Ingredients**:

- 1 pumpkin
- 2 onions
- 2 cloves of garlic
- 1 tablespoon butter
- Laminated almonds to decorate

**Directions**:

1. Cut the squash into pieces and salt and pepper. Bake the pumpkin at 180° C until it is soft. Caramelize onions over low heat with the butter. Fry the previously chopped garlic. Blend the pumpkin with the garlic and onion. Add little water if needed, so that the consistency of cream remains. Garnish with rolled almonds.

**Nutrition**: 49 Calories12g Carbs3g Fiber2g Protein

# Bean Stew

**Preparation Time**: 20 minutes

**Cooking Time**: 35 minutes

**Servings**: 4

**Ingredients**

- kg fresh beans
- 2 beautiful onions
- 200 to 400 g smoked tofu (depending on appetite)
- 5 tsp. oil neutral taste
- 2-3 tsp. chopped fresh herbs
- 10 cl of water or vegetable broth
- Salt and pepper

**Directions**:

1. Shell the beans *. Peel and finely chop the onions. Cut the smoked tofu into cubes (half a centimeter per side). Heat the oil in a sauté pan. Add the onions, sauté gently, stirring. Add the smoked tofu and mix for 5 minutes. Finally add the beans and the chopped fresh herbs chosen. Mix. Salt and pepper. Moisten water or broth. Simmer for 20 minutes, covered, stirring occasionally. Serve hot.

**Nutrition**: 206 calories15g fiber31g protein9g sugar

# Pumpkin Soup

**Preparation Time**: 10 minutes

**Cooking Time**: 45 minutes

**Servings**: 2

**Ingredients**:

- 1 medium slice of tomato
- ½ small onions
- 2 garlic cloves
- ½ plates (table) of Swiss chard
- 1 stalk of celery
- 1 tablespoon chopped parsley
- 4 small pieces of pumpkin
- 2 ½ cups of water
- 1 teaspoon light salt
- Pepper to taste
- 1 plate (table) of endive

**Directions**:

1. Peel and chop all **ingredients** Put the **ingredients** in a saucepan, except the endive. Add water, salt, and pepper. Let it cook until soft, then remove from the heat and beat in the blender until a homogeneous mixture is obtained. Add in a saucepan the broth, finely chopped endive strips and whipped whites. Cook a little more, turn off the heat and serve.

**Nutrition**: 10.1g Protein165 Calories1.06g Sodium22.7g Total Carbohydrate

# Beautifully Curried Eggplant

**Preparation Time**: 5 minutes

**Cooking Time**: 5 minutes

**Serving**: 2

**Ingredients**

- 1 piece of roasted eggplant (make sure to remove the contents from  the shell and reserve juice from about 1 lemon)
- 1 teaspoon of sea salt
- 1 teaspoon of curry powder
- Water as required
- Cooked quinoa required for **serving**

**Directions**:

1. Take a food processor and add eggplant, lemon juice, sesame oil, salt, curry powder and blend the whole mixture well. Take a small sized saucepan and place it over medium heat

2. Add the eggplant mix to your saucepan and gently warm it for about 5 minutes. Add water to thin it if required. Serve the curried eggplants over some delicious quinoa!

**Nutrition**81 Calories•2.8g Fats•14g Carbs8g Fiber

# Coconut Milk and Glazing Stir Fried Tofu

**Preparation Time**: 10 minutes

**Cooking Time**: 5 minutes

**Serving**: 4

**Ingredients**

- 1 pound of firm tofu
- 3 medium sized Zucchinis
- 3 pieces of tomatoes
- 1 piece of red bell pepper
- 1 piece of green bell pepper
- ½ a pound of green beans
- 1 to 1 and a ½ cup of fresh coconut milk
- 2 tablespoon of cold pressed extra virgin olive oil
- Sea salt as needed
- Pepper as needed
- ½ a tablespoon of curry powder
- ¼ tablespoon of ginger
- Fresh assorted selection of Herbs

**Directions**

1. Dice your tofu. Chop up your zucchinis. Chop up the bell peppers, tomatoes, beans into small portions. Take a pan and place it over medium heat, add oil and heat it up
2. Add tofu and fry them for about 2-3 minutes. Add pepper bell, beans, zucchini and stir fry for 2-3 minutes. Add tomatoes and coconut milk and stir well and cook for a while
3. Season with some ginger, salt, pepper, curry powder, and herbs. Serve with some wild rice or soba noodles

**Nutrition**210 Calories17g Fats8g Carbs3g Fiber

# Culturally Diverse Pumpkin Potato Patties

**Preparation Time**: 10 minutes

**Cooking Time**: 5 minutes

**Serving**: 2

**Ingredients**

- 1 pound of 450g pumpkin
- 1 pound of 450g potatoes

- ounce of soy 75g soy flour
- 4 tablespoons of water
- 3 tablespoons of chopped up parsley
- Sea salt as needed
- Organic salt as needed
- Just a pinch of pepper
- Cold Pressed Extra virgin olive oil

## Directions

1. Peel the skin of your pumpkin and potatoes. Take a grater and grate both of them into chunky pieces. Take a bowl and add 2 tablespoons of soy flour and 4 tablespoons of water
2. Take another bowl and add your grated potatoes and pumpkin alongside soy flour. Add flour to the mix and mix them well. Season with a bit of salt, parsley, and pepper. Take a pan and place it over medium heat. Add oil and heat it up. Prepare patties from the mixture and fry them in hot oil for about 2-3 minutes until they are brown

**Nutrition**375 Calories16g Fats46g Carbs7g Fiber

# Italian Leek Fry

**Preparation Time**:  10minutes

**Cooking Time**: 20 minutes

**Serving**: 2

## Ingredients

- 2 silvered stalks of leeks
- 2 diced up middle sized white onion
- 1 silvered Zucchini
- 2 coarsely diced up tomatoes
- 2 tablespoon of extra virgin olive oil
- 1 tablespoon of grated cheddar
- 1 teaspoon of sea salt
- 1 tablespoon of parsley
- 1 teaspoon of oregano
- ½ a teaspoon of curry powder
- Freshly ground black pepper
- ½ a cup of water

## Directions

1. Take a medium sized pan and add olive oil, heat it up over medium heat. Add onions and sauté them until lightly browned. Add  zucchinis and cook for about 3-4 minutes
2. Pour water and cover up the pan. Lower down the heat to low and let it simmer for 10 minutes

3. Add tomatoes and season with some pepper and curry powder. Cook for 10 minutes, making sure to keep the lid closed. Once done, season with some more parsley and salt. Add cheese and serve! Serve with some bread if you require your meal to have greater alkaline value!

**Nutrition**80 Calories7g Fats4g Carbs1g Fiber

# Pasta with Walnut Pesto

**Preparation Time**: 10 minutes

**Cooking Time**: 25 minutes

**Servings**: 4

**Ingredients**:

- ½ cup Walnuts
- Juice of a lime
- Sea salt
- 3 cup Fresh basil
- Avocado
- ½ cup Spelt pasta

**Directions**:

1. To start, add the basil, avocado, walnuts, lime juice, and salt to a food processor. Blend well all the **ingredients** to form a smooth sauce.
2. Next, cook your spelt pasta according to the **directions** on the packaging. Once cooked, drain, and pour into a bowl. Pour in the pesto and mix everything together. At this point, you can mix in some extra Dr. Sebi approved **ingredients** like chopped olives, chopped tomatoes, and torn basil. Enjoy.

**Nutrition**: 190 calories4g sugar18g fat

# Walnut Kale Pasta

**Preparation Time**: 12 minutes

**Cooking Time**: 20 minutes

**Servings**: 6

**Ingredients**:

- Cayenne pepper to taste
- Sea salt to taste
- 2 tbsp Avocado oil
- 1 small Chopped onion
- 1/3 cup Walnut flakes
- 1 ½ cup Spelt pasta
- 3 cups Kale

**Directions**:

1. Begin by fixing the pasta the way the package tells you to. It still needs to be "al dente."
2. Wash the kale and chop into bite-size pieces.
3. Put the avocado oil in a large skillet and slowly heat it up then add the onion. Allow the onion to cook until it has softened and turned a translucent color now put the kale into the skillet and stir to combine with onions. Add some water and cook until kale is wilted.
4. In another dry skillet, add the walnut flakes and toast gently.
5. Once the kale is wilted, add pasta, and stir well to combine.
6. Sprinkle with walnut flakes and season to taste.

**Nutrition**: 204 calories18g protein5g sugar

# Tomato Pasta

**Preparation Time**: 15 minutes

**Cooking Time**: 20 minutes

**Servings**: 4

**Ingredients**:

- 1lb Spelt pasta
- 2 tbsp Olive oil
- 1 Bell pepper
- 1 medium Zucchini
- 1 large Onion
- 1 (15 oz) can Chickpeas
- 5 Chopped tomatoes

**Directions**:

1. Start by fixing the pasta the way the package tells you to.
2. Wash and chop the zucchini, onion, bell pepper, and tomatoes. Add to a skillet along with some water.
3. "Steam fry" the vegetables until tender.
4. Drain and rinse the chickpeas. Put them in the tomato mixture and cook five minutes or until they have been warmed through.
5. Drain the pasta and divide it evenly into plates. Divide the sauce evenly and pour on the pasta. If you want the extra flavor, you can drizzle some olive oil on top and enjoy.

**Nutrition**: 116 calories9g fat13g protein

# Spicy Sesame Ginger Noodle Bowl

**Preparation Time**: 10 minutes

**Cooking Time**: 20 minutes

**Servings**: 6

**Ingredients**:

- 8 oz Spelt angel hair pasta
- 2 tbsp Sesame oil
- 1 Peeled and chopped cucumber
- 1 tsp Onion powder
- 1 tbsp Walnut butter
- 1 tbsp Tahini
- Juice of one key lime
- 1 tbsp Grated ginger
- Sea salt to taste
- Cayenne pepper to taste

**Directions**:

1. Fix the pasta as per the **directions** on the package. Drain and rinse with cool water. Leave in colander while you make the dressing.
2. Add the onion powder, ginger, lime juice, sesame oil, tahini, walnut butter, cayenne, salt, and cucumber to a small bowl. Whisk until walnut butter and tahini are incorporated together. Taste and adjust seasonings if needed.
3. Transfer the pasta in a large bowl then drizzle dressing over the top. Toss to coat.
4. You may garnish with black sesame seeds and lime wedges if desired.

**Nutrition**: 130 calories15g fiber20g protein

# Zucchini Tomato Pasta

**Preparation Time**: 10 minutes

**Cooking Time**: 25 minutes

**Servings**: 4

**Ingredients**:

- 2 Key lime wedges,
- 2 medium Zucchinis
- Sea salt to taste
- 1 tsp Basil
- 2 Chopped tomatoes
- 1 tsp Oregano
- 1 medium Chopped onion
- 2 tsp Avocado oil

**Directions**:

1. Begin by warming some avocado oil in a skillet. Add the onion to the skillet and let the onion cook until it has softened. Add in salt, oregano, basil, and tomatoes. Stir well and continue cooking until the tomatoes are soft and the **ingredients** have cooked together. This will take about four minutes.

2.  Using either a spiralizer or peeled, turn the zucchini into noodles. Divide them equally between two plates. Add one lime wedge to each plate.
3.  If you want your zucchini heated through, you can add it to the sauce for a minute. Cooking the zucchini for too long will lose some of its nutrients.
4.  When ready to eat, squeeze the lime over the pasta and enjoy.

**Nutrition**: 150 calories17g protein9g fiber

# Creamy Mushroom Pasta

**Preparation Time**: 15 minutes

**Cooking Time**: 30 minutes

**Servings**: 6

**Ingredients**:

- Cayenne pepper to taste
- 3 cups Coconut milk
- Sea salt to taste
- 3 tbsp Chickpea Flour
- 8 cups Mixed mushrooms
- 1 medium Chopped onion
- ¼ cup Avocado oil
- 1lb. Spelt pasta

**Directions**:

1.  In a large pasta pot, pour eight cups water and add a large handful of sea salt. Cook the pasta like the package states. When done, drain.
2.  While the pasta cooks, you can get the sauce ready.
3.  Warm the avocado oil in a skillet. Place the onions, mushroom, and a pinch of salt. Cook while occasionally stirring until mushrooms have softened and are slightly browned. This will take about 15 minutes. Turn the heat down after five minutes have passed.
4.  Sprinkle the flour over the mushroom mixture and stir well. Make sure everything is covered with the flour. Let this cook for about one minute. Turn the heat back on.
5.  Add in one cup of the coconut milk while constantly stirring and simmer for one minute. Break up any clumps that might have formed.
6.  Once it is totally smooth and has thickened a bit, add the rest of the coconut milk. Add some cayenne for your taste and bring the liquid to a simmer while constantly stirring.
7.  Continue cooking until the sauce has thickened one more time.
8.  Take off heat. Taste and adjust seasonings if needed.
9.  Place the cooked pasta into the sauce. Toss well to coat everything.
10. Divide into **serving** plates and enjoy.

**Nutrition**: 160 calories18g fiber24g protein

# Alkaline Blueberry and Strawberry Muffins

**Preparation Time**: 15 minutes

**Cooking Time**:  5 hours

**Servings**: 6

**Ingredients**:

- 3/4 cup quinoa flour
- 3/4 cup teff flour
- 1/2 teaspoon salt
- 1/3 cup agave
- 1 cup fresh coconut milk
- 1/4 cup strawberries, chopped
- 1/4 cup blueberries

**Directions**:

1. Place the quinoa flour, teff flour, and salt in a bowl.
2. In another bowl, combine the agave and coconut milk. Slowly pour the wet **ingredients** to the dry **ingredients**. Mix until well-combined. Stir in the berries and mix until well-combined.
3. Pour the batter in muffin pans. Place the muffin pans with the batter in the Instant Pot.
4. Close the lid but do not set the vent to the Sealing position.
5. Press the Slow Cook button and adjust the **cooking time** to 4 to 5 hours.

**Nutrition**: 271 Calories7.2g Protein36.6g Carbs4.3g Sugar11.5g Fat

# Dr. Sebi Salsa Verde

**Preparation Time**: 15 minutes

**Cooking Time**: 20 minutes

**Servings**: 2

**Ingredients**

- 1 tsp. Onion Powder
- 1/4 cup Fresh Cilantro
- Blender
- 1/2 cup Onions
- 1 pound of Tomatillos
- 1 tsp. Oregano
- Strainer
- 1 tsp. Sea Salt

**Direction**

1. Rinse the tomatillos, remove the skin, rinse again then cut in half. Set aside the cilantro then add the other **ingredients** into the saucepan. Add enough water to cover the tomatillos.
2. Set your cooker to medium-high heat then stir occasionally for 20 minutes. Thoroughly strain the **ingredients** then add cilantro and the mixture to the blender. Allow to blend for 30 seconds.

**Nutrition**: 114 calories13g fiber25g protein

# Creamy Creamed Corn

**Preparation Time**: 2 hours

**Cooking Time**: 2 hours

**Servings**: 5

**Ingredients**:

- 16 ounce of frozen corn kernels
- 1 teaspoon of salt and
- 1/2 teaspoon of ground black pepper
- 1 tablespoon honey
- 1/2 cup of vegetarian butter, unsalted
- 8-ounce of cream cheese, softened
- 1/2 cup of almond milk

**Directions**:

1. Take a 6-quarts slow cooker, grease it with a non-stick cooking spray and place **ingredients** in it. Stir properly and cover the top.  Plug in the slow cooker; adjust the **cooking time** to 4 hours and let it cook on the low heat setting or until it is cooked thoroughly.  Serve right away.

**Nutrition**: 120 Calories28g Carbohydrates2g Protein1g Fats4g Fiber

# Savory Squash & Apple Dish

**Preparation Time**: 15 minutes

**Cooking Time**: 4 hours

**Servings**: 6

**Ingredients**:

- 8 ounces of dried cranberries
- 4 medium-sized apples
- 3 pounds of butternut squash
- Half of a medium-sized white onion
- 1 tablespoon of ground cinnamon

- 1-1/2 teaspoons of ground nutmeg

**Directions**:

1. Take a 6-quarts slow cooker, grease it with a non-stick cooking spray and place the **ingredients** in it. Stir properly and cover the top. Plug in the slow cooker; adjust the **cooking time** to 4 hours and let it cook on the low heat setting or until it cooks thoroughly. Serve right away.

**Nutrition**: 210 Calories11g Carbohydrates3g Protein5g Fats6g Fiber

# Spicy Cajun Boiled Peanuts

**Preparation Time**: 15 minutes

**Cooking Time**: 8 hours

**Servings**: 15

**Ingredients**:

- 5 pounds of peanuts, raw and in shells
- 6-ounce of dry crab boil
- 4-ounce of jalapeno peppers, sliced
- 2-ounce of vegetable broth

**Directions**:

1. Take a 6-quarts slow cooker place the **ingredients** in it and cover it with water. Stir properly and cover the top. Plug in the slow cooker; adjust the **cooking time** to 8 hours and let it cook on the low heat setting or until the peanuts are soft and floats on top of the cooking liquid. Drain the nuts and serve right away.

**Nutrition**: 309 Calories5g Carbohydrates26g Fats

# Carrot and Spinach Salad

**Preparation Time**: 60 minutes

**Cooking Time**: 0 minutes

**Serving**: 4

**Ingredients**:

- 0.8 lb. baby spinach leaves
- 2 carrots, peeled, grated
- 5 tbsp. olive oil
- 4 tbsp. lemon juice
- Salt and black pepper, to taste
- 1 tsp. thyme
- 1-2 garlic cloves, minced
- ¼ tsp. olive powder

**Directions**:

1. Stir in lemon juice, olive oil, salt, pepper, onion powder, and garlic. Mix well.
2. Add carrots and spinach leaves to mixture. Toss to combine.
3. Cover the bowl with a plastic wrapper. Place it in the refrigerator for about 50 minutes before **serving**.

**Nutrition**: 215 Calories4.5g Fat54.4g Carbohydrates14g Protein

# Red Cabbage Salad

**Preparation Time**: 15 minutes

**Cooking Time**: 0 minutes

**Serving**: 4

**Ingredients**:

- 1 lb. red cabbage, thinly sliced
- 2 carrots, peeled, thinly sliced
- 2 tbsp. olive oil
- Salt and black pepper, to taste
- 2 tbsp. lemon juice
- 2 tbsp. coriander leaves, chopped
- 1 tbsp. mint leaves, chopped

**Directions**:

1. Combine cabbage, carrots, mint, and coriander. Mix in salt, pepper, lemon juice, and olive oil then toss it well. Transfer salad onto a **serving** platter.

**Nutrition**: 226 Calories5g Fat217g Carbohydrates12g Protein

# Quinoa Fruit Salad

**Preparation Time**: 15 minutes

**Cooking Time**: 0 minutes

**Serving**: 3

**Ingredients**:

- 1 lb. cooked quinoa
- 1 mango, peeled and diced
- ½ lb. strawberries, quartered
- ½ lb. blueberries
- 2 tbsp. pine nuts
- Chopped mint leaves, for garnish
- 4 tbsp. olive oil
- Zest of 1 lemon, as required

- 3 tbsp. freshly squeezed lemon juice
- 1 tbsp. date sugar

**Directions**:

1. For the vinaigrette, beat the olive oil, lemon zest, juice, and sugar in a small bowl. Set aside.
2. Mix quinoa, mango, strawberries, blueberries, and pine nuts in a large bowl. Add the lemon vinaigrette.

**Nutrition**: 490 Calories17.2g Fat77.3g Carbohydrates9.8g Protein

# Kale and Carrot Salad

**Preparation Time**: 15 minutes

**Cooking Time**: 0 minutes

**Serving**: 5

**Ingredients**:

- 0.6 lb. kale leaves, chopped
- 2 tbsp. lime juice
- 4 tbsp. olive oil
- salt and ground black pepper to taste
- 2 carrots, peeled, shredded
- 0.3 lb. red cabbage, shredded
- 1 small red onion, chopped
- 1 garlic clove, minced

**Directions**:

1. Combine kale leaves, carrots, cabbage, onion, and garlic. Mix in salt, pepper, lime juice, and olive oil. Toss to combine. Add to a **serving** bowl.

**Nutrition**: 241 Calories5g Fat42g Carbohydrates4g Protein

# Kale Salad with Lemon Vinaigrettes

**Preparation Time**: 25 minutes

**Cooking Time**: 0 minutes

**Serving**: 4

**Ingredients**:

- ½ lb. chopped kale
- 1 avocado, diced
- 0.7 lb. cooked quinoa
- ½ lb. pomegranate arils
- ½ lb. chopped pecans
- 2 tbsp. olive oil

- 1 tbsp. apple cider vinegar
- 2 tbsp. freshly squeezed Meyer lemon juice
- Zest of 1 Meyer lemon, as required
- 1 tbsp. date sugar
- 1 lb. spinach leaves

**Directions**:

1. Whisk in olive oil, apple cider vinegar, lemon juice, lemon zest, and date sugar in a small bowl. Set aside. To make the salad, place the spinach in a large bowl; Garnish with avocado, quinoa, pomegranate, pecans, and walnuts.
2. Pour the vinaigrette over the salad and stir gently.

**Nutrition**: 415 Calories4.5g Fat64.4g Carbohydrates14.7g Protein

# Wonderful Steamed Artichoke

**Preparation Time**: 5 minutes

**Cooking Time**: 4 hours

**Servings**: 4

**Ingredients**:

- 8 medium-sized artichokes, stemmed and trimmed
- 2 teaspoons of salt
- 4 tablespoons of lemon juice

**Directions**:

1. Cut 1-inch part of the artichoke from the top and place it in a 6-quarts slow cooker, facing an upright position. Using a bowl, place the lemon juice and pour in the salt until it mixes properly.
2. Pour this mixture over the artichoke and add the water to cover at least ¾ of the artichokes.
3. Cover the top, plug in the slow cooker; adjust the **cooking time** to 4 hours and let it cook on the high heat setting or until the artichokes get soft. Serve immediately.

**Nutrition**: 78 Calories17g Carbohydrates5g Protein9g Fiber

# Creamy Garlic Cauliflower Mashed Potatoes

**Preparation Time**: 1 hour

**Cooking Time**: 2 hours

**Servings**: 6

**Ingredients**:

- 30-ounce of cauliflower head, cut into florets

- 6 garlic cloves, peeled
- 1 teaspoon of salt
- 3/4 teaspoon of ground black pepper
- 1 bay leaf
- 1 tablespoon of vegetarian butter, unsalted
- 3 cups of water

**Directions**:

1. Take a 6-quarts slow cooker, grease it with a non-stick cooking spray and place the cauliflower florets into it. Except for the butter, stir in the remaining **ingredients** then mix it properly.
2. Cover the top, plug in the slow cooker; adjust the **cooking time** to 3 hours and let it cook on the high heat setting or until it is cooked thoroughly. When done, open the slow cooker, remove the bay leaf and garlic cloves.
3. Drain the cooking liquid, add the butter and let it melt. Then using an immersion blender, mash the cauliflower or until it gets creamy. Add the seasoning and serve.

**Nutrition**: 66 Calories6g Carbohydrates3g Protein4.2g Fats3g Fiber

# Healthy Pumpkin Risotto

**Preparation Time**: 45 minutes

**Cooking Time**: 1 hour

**Servings**: 4

**Ingredients**:

- 2 tablespoons of olive oil
- 1/2 cup of chopped white onion
- 1 tablespoon of minced garlic
- 2 teaspoons of salt
- 1 teaspoon of ground black pepper
- 2 teaspoons of dried sage
- 1-1/2 cups of short grain rice
- 2 cups of roasted pumpkin
- 32 fluid ounce vegetable broth

**Directions**:

1. Place a medium-sized non-stick skillet pan over an average temperature of heat, add and let it heat. Then add the onion, garlic, sage and heat it for 5 minutes or until it gets softened. Pour in the rice and continue cooking for 3 minutes.
2. Transfer this mixture to a 6-quarts slow cooker and add the remaining **ingredients** except for pumpkin seeds. Stir properly and cover the top.
3. Plug in the slow cooker; adjust the **cooking time** to 1 hour 30 minutes and let it cook on the high heat setting or until the rice gets soft. Serve right away.

**Nutrition**: 190 Calories11g Carbohydrates12g Protein10g Fats3g Fiber

# Flavorful Roasted Peppers

**Preparation Time**: 20 minutes

**Cooking Time**: 3 hours

**Servings**: 5

**Ingredients**:

- 5 medium-sized red bell pepper, cored and halved

**Directions**:

1. Take a 6-quarts slow cooker, grease it with a non-stick cooking spray and add the peppers.
2. Cover the top, plug in the slow cooker; adjust the **cooking time** to 3 hours and let it cook on the high heat setting or until the peppers are softened, stirring halfway through.
3. When done, remove the peppers from the cooker and let it cool off completely.
4. Then remove the pepper peels by tugging it from the edge or with a paring knife.
5. Serve as desired.

**Nutrition**: 5 Calories1g Carbohydrates

# Comforting Spinach and Artichoke Dip

**Preparation Time**: 25 minutes

**Cooking Time**: 2 hours

**Servings**: 8

**Ingredients**:

- 8-ounce of frozen spinach, thawed and squeezed
- 8 ounce of diced water chestnuts
- 28 ounce of cooked artichoke hearts, chopped
- 1 teaspoon of minced garlic
- 1 teaspoon of salt
- 3/4 teaspoon of ground black pepper
- 2 tablespoons of **nutrition**al yeast
- 1 cup of cashew, raw
- 2 teaspoons of whole-grain mustard paste
- 2 tablespoons of lemon juice
- 3 tablespoons of soy-mayonnaise
- 1 cup of almond milk, unsweetened

**Directions**:

1. Using a food processor, place the cashews and pulse it until the mixture looks like flour, while ensuring not to over-blend.

2. Add the garlic, salt, mustard paste, lemon juice, almond milk and mash it for 2 minutes or until it gets smooth. Place this mixture into a 6-quarts slow cooker, add the remaining **ingredients** except for the mayonnaise and stir properly.
3. Cover the top, plug in the slow cooker; adjust the **cooking time** to 4 hours and let it cook on the high heat setting. When done, open the slow cooker and pour in and stir the mayonnaise properly.
4. Add the seasoning and serve.

**Nutrition**83 Calories16g Carbohydrates4g Protein

# Alkaline Sausage Links

**Preparation Time**: 15 minutes

**Cooking Time**:  6 minutes

**Servings**: 6

**Ingredients**:

- 2 cups garbanzos beans flour
- 1 cup chopped mushrooms
- 1/2 cup chopped onions
- 1 tomato, chopped
- 1 teaspoon oregano
- 1 teaspoon sea salt
- 1 teaspoon ground sage
- 1 teaspoon dill, chopped
- 1/2 teaspoon cayenne pepper powder
- Grapeseed oil for frying

**Directions**:

1. Except for the grapeseed oil, put all the **ingredients** in a bowl. Combine all the **ingredients** with your hands. Create small logs of sausages and place inside the fridge to set for at least 30 minutes.
2. Pour oil in the Instant Pot and press the Sauté button until the oil is hot.
3. Place the sausage links carefully and cook on all sides for 3 minutes.

**Nutrition**: 266 Calories14.6g Protein44.9g Carbs8.6g Sugar4.2g Fat

# Butternut Squash Hash Browns

**Preparation Time**: 15 minutes

**Cooking Time**: 6 minutes

**Servings**: 3

**Ingredients**:

- 1/2 cup butternut squash

- 1/2 cup diced onion
- A dash of sea salt
- A dash of cayenne pepper powder
- Grapeseed oil for brushing the Instant Pot

**Directions**:

1. Shred the butternut squash and place in a bowl. Add the onion, salt, and cayenne pepper.
2. Mix until well-combined. Create small patties using the mixture. Pour grapeseed oil in the Instant Pot and press the Sauté button.
3. Place the hash brown in the Instant Pot and cook for 3 minutes on all sides.

**Nutrition**: 64 Calories0.7g Protein5.9g Carbs2.1g Sugar4.6g Fat

# Blueberry Spelt Flat Cakes

**Preparation Time**: 15 minutes

**Cooking Time**:  4 hours

**Servings**: 4

**Ingredients**:

- 2 cups spelt flour
- 1/4 teaspoon sea salt
- 1/4 cup hemp seeds
- 1 cup fresh coconut milk
- 1/2 cup spring water
- 2 tablespoons grapeseed oil
- 1/2 cup agave
- 1/2 cup blueberries

**Directions**:

1. In a bowl, mix the spelt flour, sea salt, and hemp seeds. Pour in the coconut milk, water, grapeseed oil, and agave. Stir until well-combined. Pour in the blueberries.
2. Line the Instant Pot with parchment paper. Pour the batter into the Instant Pot. Close the lid but do not set the vent to the Sealing position.
3. Press the Slow Cook button and adjust the **cooking time** to 4 hours.

**Nutrition**: 574 Calories16.1g Protein74.8g Carbs14.8g Sugar27.8g Fat

# Garlicky Broccoli

**Preparation Time**: 10 minutes

**Cooking Time**: 8 minutes

**Servings**: 2

**Ingredients**:

- 1 tablespoon olive oil
- 2 garlic cloves, minced
- 2 cups broccoli florets
- 2 tablespoons water
- salt and black pepper to taste

**Directions**:

1. Cook the oil over medium heat in a skillet and sauté the garlic for about 1 minute.
2. Add the broccoli and stir fry for 2 minutes.
3. Stir in water, salt, and black pepper and stir fry for 4-5 minutes.
4. Serve hot.

**Nutrition**: 95 Calories7.3g Total Fat148 mg Sodium7g Total Carbs2.4g Fiber

# Sautéed Kale

**Preparation Time**: 10 minutes

**Cooking Time**: 20 minutes

**Servings**: 4

**Ingredients**:

- 1 tablespoon extra-virgin olive oil
- 1 lemon, seeded and sliced thinly
- 1 onion, sliced thinly
- 3 garlic cloves, minced
- 2 pounds fresh kale, trimmed and chopped
- ½ cup scallions, chopped
- salt and black pepper to taste

**Directions**:

1. Cook the oil over medium heat in a skillet and cook the lemon slices for 5 minutes.
2. With a slotted spoon, remove the lemon slices from skillet and set aside.
3. In the same skillet, add the onion and garlic and sauté for about 5 minutes.
4. Add the kale, scallions, honey, salt, and pepper and cook for 8-10 minutes.
5. Add the lemon slices and mix until well combined. Serve hot.

**Nutrition**: 161 Calories3.6g Total Fat28.3g Total Carbs4.6g Fiber1.6g Sugar7.5g Protein

# Zucchini Burritos

**Preparation Time**: 15 minutes

**Cooking Time**: 25 minutes

**Servings**: 4

**Ingredients**:

- Sesame seeds
- 1 tbsp Tahini
- Sprouted hemp seeds handful
- Dandelion greens or amaranth handful
- 1 small Zucchini, cut into rounds
- 4 sheets Nori seaweed
- ½ Sliced mango
- Cucumber
- Sliced avocado

**Directions**:

1. Put the Nori sheets onto a cutting board. Make sure the shiny side is facing the cutting board.
2. Place all the **ingredients** onto the Nori in whatever arrangement you would like. Leave about one inch uncovered on the right side of the Nori.
3. Use both hands and begin folding the Nori from the side closest to you. Roll it over the filling.
4. Slice into two-inch thick slices and sprinkle over sesame seeds.

**Nutrition**: 118 calories5g fats13g protein

# Zucchini Bacon

**Preparation Time**: 10 minutes

**Cooking Time**: 6 minutes

**Servings**: 4

**Ingredients**:

- 3 zucchinis, sliced thinly lengthwise or into large strips
- 1/4 cup date sugar
- 1/4 cup spring water
- 1 tablespoon sea salt
- 1 tablespoon onion powder
- 1/2 teaspoon cayenne pepper powder
- 1/2 teaspoon ground ginger
- 1 tablespoon liquid smoke
- Grapeseed oil for frying

**Directions**:

1. Except for the grapeseed, put all the **ingredients** in a bowl.
2. Allow the zucchini strips to marinate for at least 2 hours in the fridge.
3. On the Instant Pot, press the Sauté button and heat the oil until it slightly smokes.
4. Fry the marinated zucchini strips for 3 minutes on each side until crispy.

**Nutrition**: 36 Calories0.64g Protein8.7g Carbs6.5g Sugar0.09g Fat

# Alkaline Spelt Bread

**Preparation Time**: 15 minutes

**Cooking Time**:  6 hours

**Servings**: 8

**Ingredients**:

- 4-1/2 cups spelt flour
- 2 teaspoons sea salt
- 2 cups spring water
- 1/4 cup agave
- Grapeseed oil for brushing the bread
- A dash of sesame seeds

**Directions**:

1. In mixing the **ingredients** use hook attachment of the mixer.
2. Sift together the spelt flour and salt in a bowl. Place in a mixer and mix for 10 seconds.
3. Add in the water and agave. Mix for 10 minutes until the dough is formed.
4. Coat the dough with grapeseed oil and place in a clean bowl. Let it rest for at least 1 hour.
5. At the bottom of the Instant Pot, line it with parchment paper.
6. Sprinkle the dough with sesame seeds and place inside the Instant Pot.
7. Close the lid but do not set the vent to the Sealing position.
8. Press the Slow Cook button and adjust the **cooking time** to 6 hours.

**Nutrition**: 331 Calories14.3g Protein68.7g Carbs6.7g Sugar2.4g Fat

# Alkaline Crustless Quiche

**Preparation Time**: 15 minutes

**Cooking Time**: 4 hours

**Servings**: 4

**Ingredients**:

- 1 cup garbanzos bean flour
- 3/4 cup fresh coconut milk
- 1 tablespoon sea salt
- 1 tablespoon oregano
- 1/4 teaspoon cayenne pepper
- 2 cups mushrooms, sliced
- 1 cup kale, chopped
- 1/2 cup white onions, chopped
- 1/2 cup yellow peppers, seeded and chopped

**Directions**:

1. Place the garbanzos bean flour, coconut milk, salt, oregano, and cayenne pepper. Mix until a smooth batter is formed.
2. Stir in the rest of the **ingredients**.
3. Place a parchment paper in the bottom of the Instant Pot and pour over the mixture.
4. Close the lid but do not set the vent to the Sealing position.
5. Press the Slow Cook button and adjust the **cooking time** to 4 hours.

**Nutrition**: 328 Calories12.1g Protein40g Carbs7.3g Sugar14.9g Fat

# Date Balls

**Preparation Time**: 10 minutes

**Cooking Time**: 30 minutes

**Serving**: 20–24

**Ingredients**

- 1 cup of pitted Dates
- 1 cup of shredded Soft-Jelly Coconut
- 1/2 cup of Sesame Seeds
- 1/2 cup of Brazil Nuts*
- 1/4 cup of Agave Syrup
- 1/2 teaspoon of Pure Sea Salt

**Directions**:

1. Add Dates, shredded Coconut, Brazil Nuts*, Agave Syrup, and Pure Sea Salt in a food processor or a blender. Blend it well for about 20–30 seconds.
2. Take a spoon of the prepared mixture in your hand and make a ball. Put Sesame Seeds in a large bowl and roll Date Balls in this mixture. Repeat steps 3 and 4 until all of the Date mixture is used.

**Nutrition**: 152 calories16g fiber20g protein

# Banana Pie

**Preparation Time**: 15 minutes

**Cooking Time**: 40 minutes plus 4 hours chilling

**Serving**: 6–8

**Ingredients**

**Crust**

- 1-1/2 cups of pitted Dates
- 1-1/2 cups of shredded Soft-Jelly Coconut
- 1/4 cup of Agave Syrup
- 1/4 teaspoon of Pure Sea Salt

**Filling**

- 6–8 Burro Bananas
- 1 cup of Homemade Hempseed Milk
- 7 ounces of Organic Creamed Unsweetened Coconut
- 4 tablespoons of Agave Syrup
- 1/8 teaspoon of Pure Sea Salt

**Directions**:

1. Add crust **ingredients** in a blender, blend them for about 30 seconds or until the ball is formed. Cover the round pie pan with parchment paper, put crust mixture inside, and spread it out. Store it in the refrigerator for 10 minutes.
2. Put all filling **ingredients** in a large bowl and mix them until well combined. Pour the filling into a pan and spread it by shaking the sides. Cover the pie with foil and put it in the freezer for about 4 hours to firm up.

**Nutrition**: 105 calories17g fiber27g protein

# Strawberry Jam

**Preparation Time**: 15 minutes

**Cooking Time**: 30 minutes

**Serving**: 2 Cups

**Ingredients**

- 4 cups of chopped Strawberries
- 2/3 cup of Agave Syrup
- 1/2 cup of Sea Moss Gel
- 3 tablespoons of Key Lime Juice

**Directions**:

1. Wash and chop all Strawberries into a bowl. Mash them to a chunky consistency.
2. Put Key Lime Juice, Strawberry mixture, and Agave Syrup in a medium saucepan and cook for 10 minutes on medium-high heat, stirring occasionally. Add Sea Moss Gel to a saucepan and cook for 5 more minutes, stirring it to dissolve evenly.
3. Remove then let it cool before using it.

**Nutrition**: 97 calories12g fiber20g protein

# Spelt Cookies

**Preparation Time**: 15 minutes

**Cooking Time**: 45 minutes

**Serving**: 24

**Ingredients**

- 1-1/2 cups of Spelt Flour
- 1-1/2 of pitted Dates
- 1-1/2 rolled Spelt Flakes
- 1 cup of Raisins
- 2/3 cup of prepared Applesauce
- 1/3 cup of Grapeseed Oil
- 1/3 cup of Agave Syrup
- 1/2 teaspoon of Pure Sea Salt
- 2 tablespoons of Sparkling Spring Water

**Directions**:

1. Add Dates, Spelt Flour, and Pure Sea Salt in a food processor and blend them well. Put prepared mixture into a bowl, add Applesauce, Spelt Flakes, Raisins, Sparkling Spring Water, Agave Syrup, and Grapeseed Oil. Mix them until well combined.
2. Preheat your oven to 350ºF then line the cookie sheet with parchment paper. Take a spoonful of the dough in your hand, form a ball, and put it on the cookie sheet. Flatten it with a fork or your fingers. Bake cookies for about 20 minutes.

**Nutrition**: 107 calories12g fiber24g protein

# Coconut Tahini Cookies

**Preparation Time**: 15 minutes

**Cooking Time**: 30 minutes

**Serving**: 8

**Ingredients**

- 1 cup of Unsweetened Coconut Flakes
- 1/4 cup of Agave Syrup
- 1 tablespoon of Homemade Tahini Butter
- 2 tablespoons of Coconut Oil
- Pinch of Pure Sea Salt

**Directions**:

1. Blend all the **ingredients** then pulse 5 times and then blend for 20 seconds until well mixed. Put prepared mixture into cupcake liners with a spoon. Freeze it for about 15–20 minutes to set coconut oil and firm up the cookies.

**Nutrition**: 105 calories24g protein12g sugar

# Teff Tahini Cookies

**Preparation Time**: 10 minutes

**Cooking Time**: 40 minutes

**Serving**: 15–18

**Ingredients**

- 1-1/4 cups of Teff Flour
- 2/3 cup of Agave Syrup
- 2/3 cup of Homemade Tahini Butter
- 1/4 cup of Grapeseed Oil
- 1/4 teaspoon of Pure Sea Salt

**Directions**:

1. Preheat your oven to 350ºF. Put Agave Syrup, Homemade Tahini Butter, and Grapeseed Oil in a bowl and mix them. Add Teff Flour and Pure Sea Salt to the mixture and blend well.
2. Line the cookie sheet with parchment paper. Take a spoonful of the dough in your hand, form a ball, and put it on the cookie sheet half an inch apart. Gently flatten it with a fork or fingers.
3. Repeat steps 4 and 5 until all the dough is used. Bake cookies for about 10–12 minutes.

**Nutrition**: 99 calories17g fiber24g protein

# Strawberry Banana Ice Cream

**Preparation time**: 10 minutes

**Cooking Time**: 4 hours

**Serving**: 5

**Ingredients**

- 1 cup of Strawberry*
- 5 quartered Baby Bananas*
- 1/2 chopped Avocado
- 1 tablespoon of Agave Syrup
- 1/4 cup of Homemade Walnut Milk

**Directions**:

1. Put all above-mentioned **ingredients** into a blender and mix them well. Taste cooked mixture. If you think it is too thick, add extra Homemade Walnut Milk**. If you want it sweeter, add extra Agave Syrup. Place the mixture in a container with a lid. Allow it to freeze for at least 5–6 hours.

**Nutrition**: 92 calories16g fiber24g protein

# Mixed Berry Mousse

**Preparation Time**: 10 minutes

**Cooking Time**: 25 minutes

**Servings**: 4

**Ingredients**:

- 1 teaspoon lemon zest

- 3 oz. raspberries and blueberries
- ¼ teaspoon vanilla essence
- 2 cups coconut cream

**Directions**:

1. Blend cream in an electric mixer until fluffy. Stir in vanilla and lemon zest. Mix well. Fold in nuts and berries. Cover the bowl with a plastic wrap. Refrigerate for 3 hours. Garnish as desired.

**Nutrition**: 265 Calories13g Total Fat1.1g Sugar0.5g Fiber

# Almond Pulp Cookies

**Preparation Time**: 5 minutes

**Cooking Time**: 10 hours.

**Servings**: 4

**Ingredients**:

- 3 cups almond pulp
- 1 Granny Smith apple
- 1-2 teaspoon cinnamon
- 2-3 tablespoons raw honey
- 1/4 cup coconut flakes

**Directions**:

1. Blend almond pulp with remaining **ingredients** in a food processor. Make small cookies out this mixture. Place them on a cookie sheet, lined with parchment paper. Place the sheet in a food dehydrator for 6 to 10 hours at 115 degrees F. Serve.

**Nutrition**: 240 Calories22.5g Total Fat14.9g Protein

# Avocado Pudding

**Preparation Time**: 10 minutes

**Cooking Time**: 0 minute

**Servings**: 2

**Ingredients**:

- 2 avocados
- 3/4-1 cup almond milk
- 1/3-1/2 cup raw cacao powder
- 1 teaspoon 100% pure organic vanilla (optional)
- 2-4 tablespoons Swerve Sweetener

**Directions**:

1.  Blend all the **ingredients** in a blender. Refrigerate for 4 hours in a container. Serve.

**Nutrition**: 609 Calories50.5g Total Fat9.69g Total Carb

# Coconut Raisins Cookies

**Preparation Time**: 10 minutes

**Cooking Time**: 10 minutes

**Servings**: 4

**Ingredients**:

- 1 1/4 cup almond flour
- 1 cup coconut flour
- 1 teaspoon baking soda
- 1/2 teaspoon Celtic sea salt
- 1 cup nut butter
- 1 cup coconut palm sugar
- 2 teaspoons vanilla
- ¼ cup almond milk
- 3/4 cup organic raisins
- 3/4 cup coconut chips or flakes

**Directions**:

1.  Set your oven to 357 degrees F. Mix flour with salt and baking soda. Blend butter with sugar until creamy then stirs in almond milk and vanilla.
2.  Mix well then stir in dry mixture. Mix until smooth. Fold in all the remaining **ingredients**. Make small cookies out this dough. Arrange the cookies on a baking sheet. Bake for 10 minutes until golden brown.

**Nutrition**: 237 Calories19.8g Total Fat0.9g Fiber17.8g Protein

# Strawberry Milkshake

**Preparation Time**: 10 minutes

**Cooking Time**: 5 minutes

**Serving**: 2

**Ingredients**

- 2 cups of Homemade Hempseed Milk
- 1 cup of frozen Strawberries
- Agave Syrup, to taste

**Directions**:

1.  Prepare and put all **ingredients** in a blender or a food processor. Blend it well until you reach a smooth consistency.

# Banana Milkshake

**Preparation time**: 10 minutes

**Cooking Time**: 5 Minutes

**Serving**: 1

**Ingredients**

- 6 frozen* Baby Bananas
- 1/4 cup of Homemade Hempseed Milk
- 1/8 teaspoon of Cloves
- 1 tablespoon of Agave Syrup

**Directions**:

1. Prepare and put all **ingredients** in a blender or a food processor. Blend it well until you reach a smooth consistency. If it is too thick, add extra Homemade Hempseed Milk.

**Nutrition**: 108 calories28g protein14g fiber

# Chocolate Crunch Bars

**Preparation Time**: 3 hours.

**Cooking Time**: 5 minutes.

**Servings**: 4

**Ingredients**:

- 1 1/2 cups sugar-free chocolate chips
- 1 cup walnut butter
- Stevia to taste
- 1/4 cup coconut oil
- 3 cups pecans, chopped

**Directions**:

1. Layer an 8—inch baking pan with parchment paper. Mix chocolate chips with butter, coconut oil, and sweetener in a bowl.
2. Melt it by heating in a microwave for 2 to 3 minutes until well mixed. Stir in nuts and seeds. Mix gently.
3. Pour this batter into the baking pan and spread evenly.
4. Refrigerate for 2 to 3 hours.
5. Slice and serve.

**Nutrition**: 316 Calories30.9g Fat8.3g Carbs6.4g Protein3.8g Fiber

# Walnut Butter Bars

**Preparation Time**: 40 minutes.

**Cooking Time**: 10 minutes.

**Servings**: 6

**Ingredients**:

- 3/4 cup coconut flour
- 2 oz. walnut butter
- 1/4 cup Swerve
- 1/2 cup walnut butter
- 1/2 teaspoon vanilla

**Directions**:

1. Combine all the **ingredients** for bars. Transfer this mixture to 6—inch small pan. Press it firmly.
2. Refrigerate for 30 minutes. Slice and serve.

**Nutrition**: 214 Calories19g Fat6.5g Carbs6.3g Protein2.1g Fiber

# Alkaline Papaya Smoothie

**Preparation Time**: 10 minutes

**Cooking Time**: 0 minutes

**Serving**: 2

**Ingredients**:

- ½ large papaya, with seeds
- 4-5 dates
- 2 burro bananas
- ½ lb. fresh spring water
- 1 tbsp. Bromide Plus Powder
- Juice of half a key lime

**Directions**:

1. To make your alkaline mineral shake, mix all the **ingredients** in the blender and blend. Add to **serving** glasses. Serve and enjoy.

**Nutrition**: 3.6g Fat1g Protein101 Calories17.1g Carbohydrates

# Cucumber and Watercress Smoothie

**Preparation Time**: 10 minutes

**Cooking Time**: 15 minutes

**Serving**: 4

**Ingredients**:

- 1½ tbsp. Dr. Sebi's Stomach Relief Herbal Tea
- 1 tbsp. tamarind pulp
- 1 seeded cucumber
- 1 fistful of watercress or wild arugula
- Juice of one key lime

**Directions**:

1. To prepare the smoothie to support the pancreas, start by boiling distilled water and add 1½ tbsp. of Dr. Sebi's Stomach Relief Herbal Tea. Alarm for about 15 minutes. Filter and let cool.
2. Mix the dough with the rest of the **ingredients** in a blender quickly.

**Nutrition**: 1.9g Total Fat1.3g Protein61 Calories9.9g Carbohydrates

# Heart-Healthy Berry Smoothie

**Preparation Time**: 15 minutes

**Cooking Time**: 0 minutes

**Serving**: 2

**Ingredients**:

- 1 tbsp. of Bromide Plus Powder
- ½ lb. strawberries
- ½ lb. blueberries
- ½ lb. blackberries
- ½ lb. raspberries
- ½ lb. walnuts

**Directions**:

1. Mix all the **ingredients** in a high-speed mixer. Add into a **serving** glass Serve and enjoy.

**Nutrition**: 5.1g Total Fat2.8g Protein83 Calories9.1g Carbohydrates

# Zucchini Relaxing Smoothie

**Preparation Time**: 15 minutes

**Cooking Time**: 10 minutes

**Serving**: 4

**Ingredients**:

- 1 zucchini, chopped
- 0.2 lb. herbal tea
- ½ lb. soft jelly coconut water

**Directions**:

1. To make your smoothie relaxed, first brew the tea according to the instructions and let it cool. Combine all **ingredients** in a blender. Blend well.  Pour into **serving** glasses and enjoy!

**Nutrition**: 0.4g Fat1.1g Protein52 Calories12.5g Carbohydrates

# Magnesium-Boosting Smoothie

**Preparation Time**: 10 minutes

**Cooking Time**: 0 minutes

**Serving**: 2

**Ingredients**:

- ½ lb. fresh spring water
- 0.7 lb. brazil nuts
- ½ burro banana
- 2 strawberries
- ½ lb. figs

**Directions**:

1. Combine all the **ingredients** in a high-speed mixer. Add more water if the mixture is too concentrated. Enjoy.

**Nutrition**: 182 Calories3g Fat40.7g Carbohydrates2.8g Protein

# Detox Smoothie

**Preparation Time**: 20 minutes

**Cooking Time**: 0 minutes

**Serving**: 4

**Ingredients**:

- ½ avocado
- ½ lb. homemade soft-jelly coconut milk
- 1 handful of "approved" greens, such as callaloo, watercress, or dandelion greens
- 1 squeeze of key lime
- 1 tsp. of Dr. Sebi's Bromide Plus Powder

**Directions**:

1. Combine all the **ingredients** in a high-speed mixer. Add more water if the mixture is too concentrated. Enjoy.

**Nutrition**: 202 Calories19.4g Fat8.8g Carbohydrates2.4g Protein

# Immunity-Boosting Smoothie

**Preparation Time**: 35 minutes

**Cooking Time**: 20 minutes

**Serving**: 2

**Ingredients**:

- 1 mango
- 1 Seville orange
- ½ lb. brewed Dr. Sebi's Immune Support Herbal Tea
- 1 tbsp. coconut oil
- 1 tbsp. date sugar or agave syrup
- 1 lime, juiced

**Directions**:

1. Boil distilled water and pour 1 half tsp. of Dr. Sebi's Immune Support Herbal Tea. Cook for about 15 minutes. Let cool, strain. Seville orange peel and mango cut into pieces.
2. Mix all **ingredients** in a high-speed mixer.  Add to **serving** glasses and enjoy!

**Nutrition**: 97 Calories3.7g Fat17.7g Carbohydrates9g Protein

# Blueberry and Strawberry Smoothie

**Preparation Time**: 5 minutes

**Cooking Time**: 0 minutes

**Serving**: 2

**Ingredients**:

- 6-7 strawberries, sliced
- ½ lb. blueberries
- ½ pint of almond milk

**Directions**:

1. Add all **ingredients** to a blender jar. Blend until smooth. Add to **serving** glasses.
2. Serve and enjoy.

**Nutrition**: 107 Calories7g Fat7g Carbohydrates4g Protein

# Mood-Boosting Smoothie

**Preparation Time**: 10 minutes

**Cooking Time**: 0 minutes

**Serving**: 2

**Ingredients**:

- ½ tsp. of Dr. Sebi's Nerve/Stress Relief Herbal Tea
- ½ lb. soft jelly coconut meat

- ½ lb. strawberries
- Date sugar, to taste

**Directions**:

1. To make a mood-boosting smoothie, start by boiling a bowl of distilled water and ½ tsp. of Dr. Sebi's Nerve/Stress Relief Herbal Tea to reduce **ingredients**.  Let stand 10-15 minutes, strain. Let it cool. Mix all **ingredients** in a blender. Blend well. Serve and enjoy.

**Nutrition**: 5.1g Fat0.9g Protein74 Calories7.6g Carbohydrates

# Cucumber and Coconut Smoothie

**Preparation Time**: 10 minutes

**Cooking Time**: 12 minutes

**Serving**: 2

**Ingredients**:

- ½ lb. soft jelly coconut water
- ½ lb. Dr. Sebi's Stomach Relief Herbal Tea
- ½ tsp. Bromide Plus Powder
- ½ cucumber, seeded
- 1 burro banana

**Directions**:

1. Make tea and let cool. Mix all the **ingredients** in a high-speed mixer and enjoy.

**Nutrition**: 1g Fat0.5g Protein46 Calories11.6g Carbohydrates

# Energy-Booting Green Smoothie

**Preparation Time**: 15 minutes

**Cooking Time**: 0 minutes

**Serving**: 4

**Ingredients**:

- 2 handfuls of greens (dandelion greens, amaranth greens, lettuce or wild arugula)
- ½ seeded cucumber
- 1 apple
- 1 burro banana
- ½ tsp. Bromide Plus Powder
- 1 tbsp. walnuts
- ½ lb. soft-jelly coconut milk

**Directions**:

1. To prepare your green smoothie, first mix all the **ingredients** in a food processor. Pour into a glass and enjoy.

**Nutrition**: 16.5g Fat2.9g Protein222 Calories19.8g Carbohydrates

# Blueberry and Apple Smoothie

**Preparation Time**: 25 minutes

**Cooking Time**: 15 minutes

**Serving**: 4

**Ingredients**:

- Brae burn apple, or another kind of organic apple
- ½-1 lb. of brazil nuts
- ½ lb. homemade walnut milk
- ½ lb. blueberries
- ½ lb. of approved greens (dandelion greens, turnip greens, watercress, etc.)
- ½ tbsp. of date sugar or agave syrup

**Directions**:

1. Combine all the **ingredients** in a high-speed mixer. Add more water if the mixture is too concentrated.

**Nutrition**: 181 Calories5.8g Fat30.2g Carbohydrates3.8g Protein

# Blueberry Pie Smoothie

**Preparation Time**: 20 minutes

**Cooking Time**: 0 minutes

**Serving**: 2

**Ingredients**:

- 1 oz. fresh blueberries
- 1 burro banana
- 1 glass coconut milk
- ½ lb. cooked amaranth
- 1 tsp. Bromide Plus Powder
- 1 tbsp. homemade walnut butter
- 1 tbsp. date sugar

**Directions**:

1. Combine all the **ingredients** in a high-speed mixer. Add more water if the mixture is too concentrated.

**Nutrition**:

413 Calories

31.9g Fat

32g Carbohydrates

5.8g Protein

# Cucumber and Carley Green Smoothie

**Preparation Time**: 10 minutes

**Cooking Time**: 0 minutes

**Serving**: 4

**Ingredients**:

- 1 lb. soft jelly coconut water
- 4 seeded cucumbers
- 2-3 key limes
- 1 bunch basil or sweet basil leaves
- ½ tsp. Bromide Plus Powder

**Directions**:

1. Mix cucumbers, basil, and lime. If you don't have a juicer, treat them in a grinder with sweet coconut jelly. Transfer in a tall glass and stir  in coconut water to make it smooth and add powdered bromide. Mix well and enjoy.

**Nutrition**: 141 Calories7.4g Fat14.2g Carbohydrates5g Protein

# Super Hydrating Smoothie

**Preparation Time**: 10 minutes

**Cooking Time**: 0 minutes

**Serving**: 4

**Ingredients**:

- ½ lb. watermelon
- ½ lb. raspberries
- ¼ seeded cucumber
- 1 key lime, juiced
- ½ lb. soft jelly coconut water

**Directions**:

1. To make the "Super Hydration" smoothie, peel the cucumber and cut it into small pieces. Mix all the **ingredients** in a fast blender. Let cool to drink. Enjoy.

**Nutrition**: 41 Calories6g Fat9.3g Carbohydrates8g Protein

# Lettuce and Ginger Detox Smoothie

**Preparation Time**: 5 minutes

**Cooking Time**: 0 minute

**Servings**: 2

**Ingredients**

- 1 cup of coconut water
- 2 cups chopped Romaine lettuce
- 1 small banana, peeled
- 1 cup ginger tea, cooled
- 6 tablespoons key lime juice
- ½ cup whole blueberries, fresh

**Directions**:

1. Take a high-powered blender, switch it on, and then place all the **ingredients** inside, in order. Close blender then pulses at high speed for 1 minute.

**Nutrition**: 160 Calories36.4g Carbohydrates0.8g Fat5g Fiber2g Protein

# Strawberry and Dates Smoothie

**Preparation Time**: 5 minutes

**Cooking Time**: 0 minute

**Servings**: 2

**Ingredients**

- 4 cups spring water
- 2 small bananas, peeled
- 5 whole strawberries
- 3 Medjool dates, pitted

**Directions**:

1. Take a high-powered blender, switch it on, and then place all the **ingredients** inside, in order. Close blender then pulses at high speed for 1 minute.

**Nutrition**: 219 Calories51.4g Carbohydrates0.8g Fat6.4g Fiber1.6g Protein

# Kale and Ginger Smoothie

**Preparation Time**: 5 minutes

**Cooking Time**: 0 minute

**Servings**: 2

**Ingredients**

- 2 cups spring water
- 1 cup kale leaves, fresh
- ¼ cup key lime juice
- 1 medium fresh apple, cored
- inch piece of ginger, fresh
- 1 cup sliced cucumber, fresh
- 1 tablespoon of sea moss gel

**Directions**:

1. Take a high-powered blender, switch it on, and then place all the **ingredients** inside, in order.
2. Close blender then pulses at high speed for 1 minute.

**Nutrition**65.5 Calories14.7g Carbohydrates0.4g Fat3.2g Fiber0.7g Protein

# Arugula and Cucumber Smoothie

**Preparation Time**: 5 minutes

**Cooking Time**: 0 minute

**Servings**: 2

**Ingredients**

- 2 cups of spring water
- 1 large bunch of callaloo, fresh
- ¼ cup of lime juice
- 1 cup diced cucumber, fresh
- 1 large bunch of arugulas, fresh
- ¼ of a honeydew, fresh
- inch piece of ginger, fresh
- 1 pear, destemmed, diced
- 6 Medjool dates, pitted
- 1 tablespoon of sea moss gel

**Directions**:

1. Take a high-powered blender, switch it on, and then place all the **ingredients** inside, in order.
2. Close blender then pulses at high speed for 1 minute.

**Nutrition**369 Calories85g Carbohydrates0.8g Fat16.1g Fiber5.5g Protein

# Dandelion and Watercress Smoothie

**Preparation Time**: 5 minutes

**Cooking Time**: 0 minute

**Servings**: 2

**Ingredients**

- 2 cups spring water
- 1 large bunch of dandelion greens, fresh
- ¼ cup key lime juice
- 1 cup of watercress, fresh
- 3 baby bananas, peeled
- ½ cup fresh blueberries
- inch piece of ginger, fresh
- 6 Medjool dates, pitted
- 1 tablespoon burdock root powder

**Directions**:

1. Take a high-powered blender, switch it on, and then place all the **ingredients** inside, in order.
2. Close blender then pulses at high speed for 1 minute.

**Nutrition**418.5 Calories96.3g Carbohydrates1.4g Fat13.6g Fiber5.2g Protein